OpenStack Orchestration

Exploit the power of dynamic cloud formation and autoscaling features to fully implement OpenStack Orchestration

Adnan Ahmed Siddiqui

[PACKT] open source*
PUBLISHING   community experience distilled

BIRMINGHAM - MUMBAI

OpenStack Orchestration

First published: October 2015

Production reference: 1201015

Published by Packt Publishing Ltd.
Livery Place
35 Livery Street
Birmingham B3 2PB, UK.

ISBN 978-1-78355-165-1

www.packtpub.com

Credits

Author
Adnan Ahmed Siddiqui

Reviewers
Mostafa A. Hamid

Maksym Lobur

Sreedhar Varma

Commissioning Editor
Neil Alexander

Acquisition Editor
Kevin Colaco

Content Development Editor
Dharmesh Parmar

Technical Editor
Siddhi Rane

Copy Editor
Janbal Dharmaraj

Project Coordinator
Harshal Ved

Proofreader
Safis Editing

Indexer
Priya Sane

Graphics
Disha Haria

Abhinash Sahu

Production Coordinator
Shantanu N. Zagade

Cover Work
Shantanu N. Zagade

About the Author

Adnan Ahmed Siddiqui is an innovative and results-driven leader with over 8 years of success. He is focused on achieving exceptional results in highly competitive environments that demand continuous improvements. He has a proven ability to architect, design, develop, and deliver cost-effective, high-performance technology solutions to meet challenging business demands. Adnan is competent in Information Lifecycle Management (ILM) and Service Delivery Lifecycle (SDLC), covering business case development, team and project management, delivery, implementation, and support. He provides consultancy and advising to various organizations in the USA and Middle East regions in OpenStack, AWS, Citrix, and Microsoft solutions.

He is a founder and CEO of CloudDall INC (`www.clouddall.com`), a successful company that helps organizations worldwide rapidly migrate their IT infrastructure to the cloud, and IKT Technologies (`www.iktechnologies.com`). Their business provisioning includes public clouds, hybrid clouds, DaaS (Desktop as a Service), backup and archive, disaster recovery, and customized storage services. CloudDall provides subscription-based services tailored to fit a range of business models resulting in reduced cost, enhanced security, control, and productivity.

In addition to these achievements, he holds a Computer Engineer degree and these certifications: Red Hat Certified Engineer (RHCSA), AWS Certified Solution Architect, Citrix Certified Enterprise Engineer for Virtualization (CCEE), Microsoft Certified Technology Specialist (MCTS), Microsoft Certified Information Technology Professional (MCITP), and Microsoft Certified System Engineer (MCSE). He has also been a Microsoft Certified Trainer (MCT) for 6 years.

About the Reviewers

Mostafa A. Hamid is a CISSP (2013), CEH v8, MCSD, IBM RUP Architect, and MCP (SUNY Potsdam USA).

He is also certified in PHP, JavaScript, Backbone, Java, Spring, Node.js, and XML web services (SUNY Potsdam, USA).

He has a bachelor's degree in management information systems (Modern Academy for Computer Science and Management Technology).

He is also certified in Java (The American University in Cairo).

He has been a technical support at Hilton, a technical support at United Systems, an IT manager at Media Plans, an ICT and IT teacher and software engineer at MOIS, a software engineer at Wasaq, and a computer programmer at Advanced Security Systems.

He is the technical reviewer of *OpenStack Essentials* and *Learning OpenStack Networking (Neutron)*, both by Packt Publishing, and the author of *OOP in PHP and MVC* and *Linux for System Administrators and DevOps* at BookBoon.com.

> Thanks for Manon Niazi, the Deutschlander, I still remember the college days. Thanks go out to my family, special thanks to the author, and of course immense thanks to the Packt Publishing team (especially, Harshal Ved, the project coordinator).

Maksym Lobur is an enthusiastic OpenStack hacker. He has worked with the technology since 2013, starting with Grizzly. He has been involved in almost all key OpenStack components such as Nova, Glance, Neutron, and Heat, and was a member of the Ironic core team during the Icehouse cycle.

Currently, he adopts OpenStack for massive telecom companies, on behalf of a private company. They are one of the top-five contributors to OpenStack worldwide.

www.PacktPub.com

Support files, eBooks, discount offers, and more

For support files and downloads related to your book, please visit www.PacktPub.com.

Did you know that Packt offers eBook versions of every book published, with PDF and ePub files available? You can upgrade to the eBook version at www.PacktPub.com and as a print book customer, you are entitled to a discount on the eBook copy. Get in touch with us at service@packtpub.com for more details.

At www.PacktPub.com, you can also read a collection of free technical articles, sign up for a range of free newsletters and receive exclusive discounts and offers on Packt books and eBooks.

https://www2.packtpub.com/books/subscription/packtlib

Do you need instant solutions to your IT questions? PacktLib is Packt's online digital book library. Here, you can search, access, and read Packt's entire library of books.

Why subscribe?

- Fully searchable across every book published by Packt
- Copy and paste, print, and bookmark content
- On demand and accessible via a web browser

Free access for Packt account holders

If you have an account with Packt at www.PacktPub.com, you can use this to access PacktLib today and view 9 entirely free books. Simply use your login credentials for immediate access.

Table of Contents

Preface

The OpenStack Orchestration program aims to create a human and machine-accessible service that manages the entire life cycle of infrastructure and applications within OpenStack clouds. Heat is the cloud orchestration service for the OpenStack framework. It implements an orchestration engine to launch multiple composite cloud applications based on templates in the form of text files that can be treated like code. It is the most popular and a still-emerging IaaS cloud framework.

This book focuses on setting up and using one of the most important services in OpenStack Orchestration, Heat. First, the book introduces you to the orchestration service for OpenStack to help you understand the uses of the templating mechanism, complex control groups of cloud resources, and huge potential and multiple-use cases. It then moves on to the topology and orchestration specification for cloud applications and standards, before introducing the most popular IaaS cloud framework, Heat. You will get to grips with the standards used in Heat, an overview and a roadmap, the architecture and CLI, the Heat API, the Heat engine, the CloudWatch API, scaling principles, JeOS, and the installation and configuration of Heat. I'll wrap up by giving you some insights into troubleshooting for OpenStack.

With easy-to-follow, step-by-step instructions and supporting images, you will be able to manage OpenStack operations by implementing the orchestration services of Heat.

What this book covers

Chapter 1, Getting Started with the Orchestration Service for OpenStack, introduces OpenStack and provides an overview of OpenStack components.

Chapter 2, The OpenStack Architecture, focuses on the detailed architecture of OpenStack and its Heat components.

Chapter 3, *Stack Group of Connected Cloud Resources*, attempts to study the basics of Heat stacks and templates and discuss the autoscaling and high-availability mechanisms supported by Heat.

Chapter 4, *Installation and Configuration of the Orchestration Service*, installs the OpenStack Orchestration service, Heat. It will also show you how to write a simple template by creating a stack.

Chapter 5, *Working with Heat*, explores the architecture of Heat in further detail. It discusses the basic architecture of Heat and the main components that build up the Orchestration service for OpenStack. It also covers the command-line arguments accepted by Heat CLI. It explains the message flow for Heat. It also explores the architecture of Heat in further detail. It focuses on the following topics: the standards used in Heat, the Heat overview and roadmap, the Heat basics, architecture and CLI, the Heat basic workflow, the Heat API, the Heat engine, the Heat CloudWatch API, and Heat autoscaling principles.

Chapter 6, *Managing Heat*, covers the installation of DevStack with Heat support. We explore Heat functionality in detail. It also discusses the basic architecture of Heat and the main components that build up the Orchestration service for OpenStack. Then, it covers the command-line arguments accepted by Heat CLI.

Chapter 7, *Troubleshooting Heat*, focuses on troubleshooting the issues encountered when using Heat. It covers the most frequently occurring issues and discusses the possible solutions for them.

What you need for this book

You will need OpenStack (Juno or Kilo). Also, you will need 1.2 Ghz CPU, 1 GB RAM, 40 GB HDD, and 2 X NIC cards. Finally, you will need Ubuntu 14.04 LTS.

Who this book is for

If you are a system engineer, system administrator, cloud administrator, or a cloud engineer, then this book is for you. You should have a background of working in a Linux-based setup. Any knowledge of OpenStack-based cloud infrastructure will help you create wonders using this book.

Conventions

In this book, you will find a number of text styles that distinguish between different kinds of information. Here are some examples of these styles and an explanation of their meaning.

Code words in text, database table names, folder names, filenames, file extensions, pathnames, dummy URLs, user input, and Twitter handles are shown as follows: "All available roles for trustor will be assigned to the trustee if no specific roles are mentioned in the `heat.conf` file."

A block of code is set as follows:

```
heat_template_version: 2013-05-23
description: Template that deploys single compute node.
resources:
my_compute-01:
type: OS::Nova::Server
properties:
key_name: my_key
image: F18-x86_64-cfntools
flavor: m1.small
```

Any command-line input or output is written as follows:

```
keystone endpoint-create --service-id $(keystone service-list | awk '/
cloudformation / {print $2}' --public http://localhost:8000/v2/%\(tenant_
id\)s --region regionOne
```

New terms and **important words** are shown in bold.

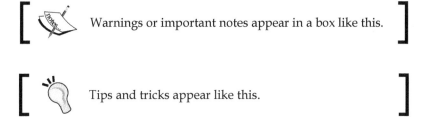

> Warnings or important notes appear in a box like this.

> Tips and tricks appear like this.

Reader feedback

Feedback from our readers is always welcome. Let us know what you think about this book — what you liked or disliked. Reader feedback is important for us as it helps us develop titles that you will really get the most out of.

To send us general feedback, simply e-mail feedback@packtpub.com, and mention the book's title in the subject of your message.

If there is a topic that you have expertise in and you are interested in either writing or contributing to a book, see our author guide at www.packtpub.com/authors.

Customer support

Now that you are the proud owner of a Packt book, we have a number of things to help you to get the most from your purchase.

Errata

Although we have taken every care to ensure the accuracy of our content, mistakes do happen. If you find a mistake in one of our books—maybe a mistake in the text or the code—we would be grateful if you could report this to us. By doing so, you can save other readers from frustration and help us improve subsequent versions of this book. If you find any errata, please report them by visiting http://www.packtpub. com/submit-errata, selecting your book, clicking on the **Errata Submission Form** link, and entering the details of your errata. Once your errata are verified, your submission will be accepted and the errata will be uploaded to our website or added to any list of existing errata under the Errata section of that title.

To view the previously submitted errata, go to https://www.packtpub.com/books/ content/support and enter the name of the book in the search field. The required information will appear under the **Errata** section.

Piracy

Piracy of copyrighted material on the Internet is an ongoing problem across all media. At Packt, we take the protection of our copyright and licenses very seriously. If you come across any illegal copies of our works in any form on the Internet, please provide us with the location address or website name immediately so that we can pursue a remedy.

Please contact us at copyright@packtpub.com with a link to the suspected pirated material.

We appreciate your help in protecting our authors and our ability to bring you valuable content.

Questions

If you have a problem with any aspect of this book, you can contact us at questions@packtpub.com, and we will do our best to address the problem.

1
Getting Started with the Orchestration Service for OpenStack

OpenStack is an open source cloud computing platform that offers mainly an **Infrastructure as a Service (IaaS)** solution and several service features such as scalability, high availability, and redundancy. It was started as a joint project by NASA and Rackspace in 2010. OpenStack is a combination of several independent components that are integrated with each user using an API. A non-profit corporate organization called OpenStack Foundation was established in the year 2012, which is responsible for maintaining the versioning and development of OpenStack.

The following are the objectives that we will cover in this chapter:

- The OpenStack architecture
- The Orchestration service of OpenStack
- The Heat workflow
- The Orchestration authorization model
- Stack domain users

Introduction to the OpenStack architecture

Several independent applications (also called **projects**) are responsible for the formation of OpenStack. These applications are discussed in the following sections.

Horizon

Horizon is the web-based control panel that provides an interface (or a dashboard) to control and carry out administrative activities in the cloud environment. It provides web-based options to interact with other components of OpenStack. New virtual machine instances can be launched using this interface. Not only this but also several other resources such as disk volumes, floating IP addresses, and so on can be managed using this interface. This project was named as Horizon.

Nova

Nova is the compute service component of the OpenStack framework that is responsible for maintaining the life cycle of virtual machines. This includes spawning of new virtual machines, stopping, restarting, and decommissioning of virtual machines.

Neutron

Neutron is the component of OpenStack that offers networking services, including LAN subnet management, VLAN management, and bridging services to be used by the virtual machine instances. It also includes the Open vSwitch application that provides an SDN-enabled forwarding device.

Swift

The Swift component of OpenStack is responsible for providing object storage services.

Object storage is a storage type where data is stored in the form of objects (data and associated metadata). It also provides an API to access and store data.

Cinder

This Cinder component of OpenStack offers block storage services. This is used by the virtual machine instances as disk volumes.

Keystone

Keystone is the component of OpenStack that provides authentication and authorization services to other components of OpenStack as well as individual users or tenants.

Glance

Glance provides disk imaging service to the virtual machine instances of OpenStack. Disk images can be used to create new disk volumes and virtual machine instances.

Ceilometer

Ceilometer is the metering service provider for OpenStack. It monitors and records several performance metrics for OpenStack components that include CPU load, CPU utilization, memory utilization, disk volume utilization, and so on.

Heat

Heat is the component of OpenStack with provides orchestration and configuration service for OpenStack components and resources. It can be used in combination with the Ceilometer component to achieve autoscalability and high availability.

Heat supports standards such as **TOSCA (Topology and Orchestration Specification for Cloud Applications)** and Amazon CloudFormation.

Trove

The Trove component of OpenStack provides a **Database as a Service (DBaaS)** solution. Both relational as well as nonrelational database engines are supported by Trove.

The Orchestration service for OpenStack

Orchestration is a main feature provided and supported by OpenStack. It is used to orchestrate cloud resources, including applications, disk resources, IP addresses, load balancers, and so on.

As discussed in the earlier sections of this chapter, the OpenStack component that is responsible for managing the orchestration services in OpenStack is Heat.

Heat contains a template engine that supports text files where cloud resources are defined. These text files are defined in a special format compatible with Amazon CloudFormation. A new OpenStack native standard has also been developed for providing templates for Orchestration called **HOT (Heat Orchestration Template)**.

Heat provides two types of clients including a command-line client and a web-based client integrated into the OpenStack dashboard.

The Orchestration project (Heat) itself is composed of several subcomponents. These subcomponents are listed as follows:

- Heat
- heat-engine
- heat-api
- heat api-cfn

Heat uses the term "stack" to define a group of services, resources, parameters inputs, constraints, and dependencies. A stack can be defined using a text file; however, the important point is to use the correct format. The JSON format used by AWS CloudFormation is also supported by Heat.

The Heat workflow

As already mentioned in the previous sections of this chapter, Heat provides two types of interfaces, including a web-based interface integrated into the OpenStack dashboard and also a **command-line interface (CLI)**, which can be used from inside a Linux shell.

The interfaces use the heat-api to send commands to the Heat engine via the messaging service (for example RabbitMQ). A metering service such as Ceilometer or CloudWatch API is used to monitor the performance of resources in the stack. These monitoring/metering services are used to trigger actions upon reaching a certain threshold. An example of this could be automatically launching a redundant web server behind a load balancer when the CPU load on the primary web server reaches above 90 percent.

The Orchestration authorization model

The Heat component of OpenStack uses an authorization model composed of mainly two types:

- Password-based authorization
- Authorization based on OpenStack identity trusts

This process is known as Orchestration authorization.

Password authorization

In this type of authorization, a password is expected from the user. This password must match with the password stored in a database by the Heat engine in an encrypted form.

The following are the steps used to generate a username/password:

1. A request is made to the Heat engine for a token or an authorization password. Normally, the Heat command-line client or the dashboard is used.

2. The validation checks will fail if the stack contains any resources under deferred operations. If everything is normal, then a username/password is provided.

3. The username/password are stored in the database in encrypted form.

In some cases, the Heat engine, after obtaining the credentials, requests another token on the user's behalf, and thereafter, access to all the roles of the stack owner are provided.

Keystone trusts authorization

Keystone trusts are extensions to OpenStack identity services that are used for enabling delegation of resources. The trustor and the trustee are the two delegates used in this method. The trustor is the user who delegates and the trustee is the user who is being delegated. The following information from the trustor is required by the identity service to delegate a trustee:

- The ID of the trustee (user to be delegated, in case of Heat, it will be the Heat user)

- The roles to be delegated (the roles are configured using the Heat configuration file, for example, to launch a new instance to achieve auto-scaling in case of reaching a threshold)

Trusts authorization execution

The creation of a stack via an API request step can be followed to execute a trust based authorization.

A token is used to create a trust between the stack owner (the **trustor**) and the Heat service user (also known as the **trustee** in this case). A special role is delegated. This role must be predefined in the `trusts_delegated_roles` list inside the `heat.conf` file.

By default, all the available roles for the trustor are set to be available for the trustee if it is not modified using a local RBAC policy.

This trust ID is stored in an encrypted form in the database. This trust ID is retrieved from the database when an operation is required.

The authorization model configuration

Heat used to support the password-based authorization until the kilo version of OpenStack was released. Using the kilo version of OpenStack, the following changes can be made to enable trusts-based authorization in the Heat configuration file:

- The default setting in `heat.conf`:

  ```
  deferred_auth_method=password
  ```

- To be replaced for enabling trusts-based authentication:

  ```
  deferred_auth_method=trusts
  ```

- The following parameters need to be set to specify trustor roles:

  ```
  trusts_delegated_roles =
  ```

As mentioned earlier, all available roles for the trustor will be assigned to the trustee if no specific roles are mentioned in the `heat.conf` file.

Stack domain users

The Heat stack domain user is used to authorize a user to carry out certain operations inside a virtual machine.

Agents running inside virtual machine instances are provided with metadata. These agents repot and share the performance statistics of the VM on which they are running.

They use this metadata to apply any changes or some sort of configuration expressed in the metadata.

A signal is passed to the Heat engine when an event is completed successfully or with the failed status. A typical example can be to generate an alert when the installation of an application is completed on a specific virtual machine after its first reboot.

Heat provides features for encapsulating all the stack-defined users into a separate domain. This domain is usually created to store the information related to the Heat service. A domain admin is created, which is used by Heat for the management of the stack-domain users.

Configuring stack domain users

The following procedure is used to configure stack domain users:

1. A new domain is created using keystone (OpenStack Identity service). Usually, the domain name is set to Heat. This ID is configured in the `heat.conf` file against the parameter `stack_user_domain`.

2. A new user is created using keystone with permissions to create and delete projects and users. This newly defined user must belong to the domain created in step 1.

3. The user created in step 2 (along with the password) is configured in `heat.conf` against the parameters: `stack_domain_admin` and `stack_domain_admin_password`.

This user is used to maintain the stack domain users on behalf of stack owners. As the `heat_domain_admin` user is only allowed access to the Heat domain, the risk of unwanted access to other domains is limited.

The following are the commands and the steps necessary to set up domain users:

1. A domain is created using the following command:

    ```
    $ openstack --os-identity-api-version=3   --os-auth-url
    http://192.168.5.38:35357/v3\

    --os-username admin --os-password ADMIN --os-project-name admin
    domain create heat \

    --description "Domain For HEAT Projects and Users"
    ```

Here $OS_TOKEN refers to a token that must be a valid token.

This will return a domain ID that will be referred to as $HEAT_DOMAIN_ID in the next step.

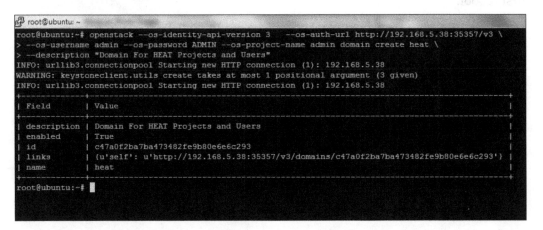

2. Next, a user will be created within the domain created in step 1:

```
$ openstack  user create heat_domain_admin \
--os-identity-api-version=3  \
--os-auth-url  http://192.168.5.38:35357/v3 \
--os-username=admin --os-password=ADMIN \
--os-project-name=admin \
--domain heat \
--description "Admin for HEAT domain"\
```

This will return a domain admin ID, which will be used in the next step.

```
root@ubuntu: ~
root@ubuntu:~# openstack  user create heat_domain_admin \
> --os-identity-api-version=3  \
> --os-auth-url  http://192.168.5.38:35357/v3 \
> --os-username=admin --os-password=ADMIN \
> --os-project-name=admin \
> --domain heat \
> --description "Admin for HEAT domain"\
INFO: urllib3.connectionpool Starting new HTTP connection (1): 192.168.5.38
INFO: urllib3.connectionpool Starting new HTTP connection (1): 192.168.5.38
INFO: urllib3.connectionpool Starting new HTTP connection (1): 192.168.5.38
WARNING: keystoneclient.utils create takes at most 1 positional argument (2 given)
INFO: urllib3.connectionpool Starting new HTTP connection (1): 192.168.5.38
+-------------+-------------------------------------------------------------------------------+
| Field       | Value                                                                         |
+-------------+-------------------------------------------------------------------------------+
| description | Admin for HEAT domain                                                         |
| domain_id   | c47a0f2ba7ba473482fe9b80e6e6c293                                              |
| enabled     | True                                                                          |
| id          | 12cc7251b9bb40359ff8050f0aa193db                                             |
| links       | {u'self': u'http://192.168.5.38:35357/v3/users/12cc7251b9bb40359ff8050f0aa193db'} |
| name        | heat_domain_admin                                                             |
+-------------+-------------------------------------------------------------------------------+
root@ubuntu:~#
```

3. Next, the newly created user in step 2 is assigned the role of domain admin:

```
$ openstack role add admin \
--user heat_domain_admin \
--os-identity-api-version=3   \
--os-auth-url  http://192.168.5.38:35357/v3 \
--os-username=admin \
--os-password=ADMIN \
--os-project-name=admin \
--domain heat
```

We'll get the output shown in the following screenshot for this command:

```
root@ubuntu:~# openstack role add admin \
> --user heat_domain_admin \
> --os-identity-api-version=3  \
> --os-auth-url  http://192.168.5.38:35357/v3 \
> --os-username=admin \
> --os-password=ADMIN \
> --os-project-name=admin \
> --domain heat
INFO: urllib3.connectionpool Starting new HTTP connection (1): 192.168.5.38
INFO: urllib3.connectionpool Starting new HTTP connection (1): 192.168.5.38
INFO: urllib3.connectionpool Starting new HTTP connection (1): 192.168.5.38
INFO: urllib3.connectionpool Starting new HTTP connection (1): 192.168.5.38
INFO: urllib3.connectionpool Starting new HTTP connection (1): 192.168.5.38
INFO: urllib3.connectionpool Starting new HTTP connection (1): 192.168.5.38
INFO: urllib3.connectionpool Starting new HTTP connection (1): 192.168.5.38
INFO: urllib3.connectionpool Starting new HTTP connection (1): 192.168.5.38
root@ubuntu:~#
```

The information such as domain ID, username, and password is needed to be configured against the relevant parameters in heat.conf.

Creating a stack

The following are the steps needed to create a sample stack:

1. If the stack contains any resources that require creation of a "stack domain user", then a new "stack domain project" in the "Heat" domain is created.

2. A new user is created under "stack domain project" by Heat if it is required. From an authentication perspective, this user is completely separate and also unrelated to the "stack owner's project."

While processing API requests, an internal lookup is made by Heat Orchestration to grant the required privileges to the user for both the stack owner's project as well as the stack domain project. These privileges are controlled by the policy.json file.

Summary

In this chapter, we learned about OpenStack, the open source cloud platform that offers IaaS features. OpenStack is made of several components, including Horizon (dashboard service), Nova (compute service), Neutron (networking service), Cinder (block storage service), Swift (object storage service), Glance (shared image service), Keystone (identify service), Ceilometer (telemetering service), Heat (Orchestration service), and Trove (database as a service). We also learned that Heat is the Orchestration service for OpenStack. We learned about the Heat authorization models, including password authorization, keystone trust authorization, and how these models work.

2

The OpenStack Architecture

In the previous chapter, we introduced OpenStack and described an overview of OpenStack components. We will focus on the detailed architecture of OpenStack and its Heat component in this chapter. The learning objectives of this chapter are:

- The OpenStack architecture
- **Topology and Orchestration Specification for Cloud Applications(TOSCA)**: Heat ideas and standards
- The logical architecture
- The example architecture
- The basic architecture with OpenStack networking

Components of OpenStack

OpenStack is an **Infrastructure as a Service (IaaS)** platform that is composed of several individual components or projects. These individual components communicate with each other using an **application programming interface(API)**. This makes it possible to install these components on either a single machine or several machines connected to each other on IP layer.

These individual components have already been briefly discussed in *Chapter 1, Getting Started with the Orchestration Service for OpenStack*; therefore, we will not repeat them again in this chapter. However, we will explain how these components can be integrated with each other using OpenStack API and IP connectivity.

The following diagram shows the main components of OpenStack installed on the three nodes:

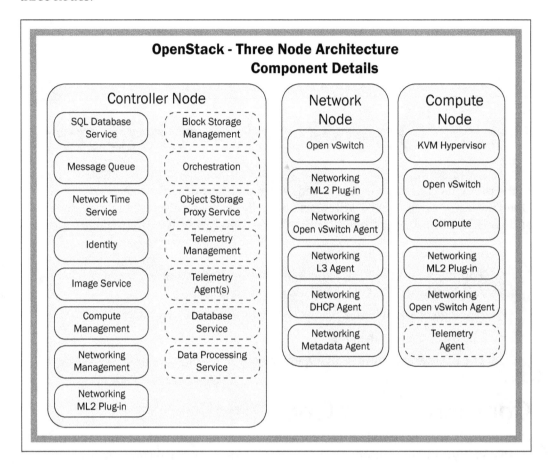

OpenStack node types

In the following table, we will describe the node types that constitute an OpenStack cloud:

Type	Description
Controller	The OpenStack controller node is used to perform the control operations in an OpenStack cloud environment. The main components running on a compute node are: Identity service (Keystone) Image service (Glance) Management functions of compute (Nova) Networking (Neutron) Dashboard (Horizon) It may also include the following optional OpenStack components: Block storage Object storage Orchestration Telemetry Besides the preceding core required and optional packages, it also includes some helper packages or applications including: Database (MySQL or other) Network Time Protocol (NTP)
Compute	This is the node which runs the virtual machines in a hypervisor portion. OpenStack uses the KVM hypervisor by default. Besides the hypervisor portion, the compute node also runs the agents for networking services that provide connectivity to internal and external networks. More than one compute nodes can be supported in an OpenStack environment. It may also have a connectivity path to storage networks for efficient communication.
Storage	The storage nodes are used to cater for the storage requirements for the cloud. This includes all virtual disk images and the virtual disks in the form of block devices. The filesystem on storage nodes can be GlusterFS or DRBD to achieve high availability and scalability.
Network	This node is mainly running the OpenStack networking services. It includes the SDN part for OpenStack that is based on open switch. The network node is responsible for providing switching, routing, IP address assignment using DHCP and NAT facilities to the OpenStack environment. The Internet connectivity for the OpenStack environment is also controlled by this node.

The OpenStack logical architecture

The following diagram shows a logical architecture of the OpenStack cloud environment. Different OpenStack components are displayed in the diagram according to their functionality and the service being provided by each service.

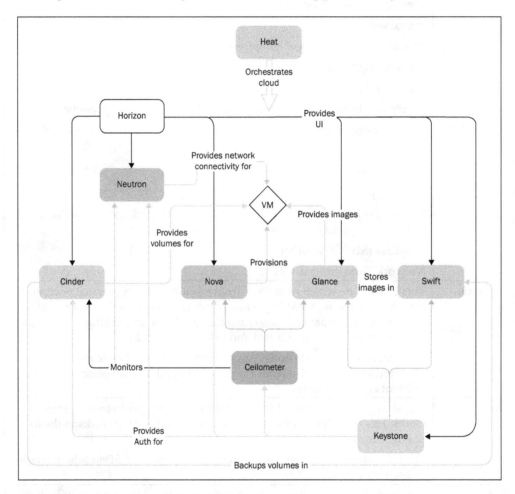

TOSCA – Heat ideas and standards

Topology and Orchestration Specification for Cloud Applications (TOSCA) has emerged as a standard orchestration and deployment framework for cloud systems. This standard has been adopted by OpenStack for their orchestration project named Heat. Heat fully supports TOSCA and offers features for materializing the design topology and dynamically scales resources according to the requirements of the applications.

Heat supports text files called **templates** for describing cloud infrastructure or the applications composing the cloud. The cloud infrastructure or bundle of components composing the cloud is called **stack** in the Heat terminology. The template format supported by Heat is the same as the AWS CloudFormation template. Heat supports the OpenStack native REST API (HOT) as well as the CloudFormation compatible query API.

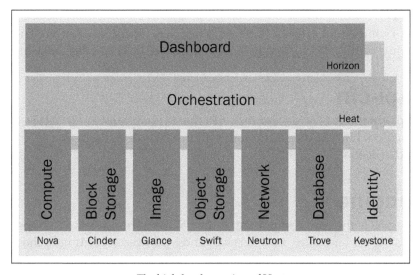

The high-level overview of Heat

Using Heat templates, resource types can be defined, which include instances, floating IPs, volumes, security groups, and users. This also supports some advanced features, including high availability, instance autoscaling, and nested stacks.

Heat components

The following are the main components for the Heat orchestration framework:

- The Heat CLI
- heat-api
- heat-api-cfn
- heat-engine
- **Heat Orchestration Template (HOT)**

The Heat CLI

The Heat CLI is the command-line tool for Heat. It interacts with heat-api to run AWS CloudFormation commands; or otherwise, it can directly run REST API commands for Heat.

heat-api

The heat-api component offers a REST API, which is OpenStack native. To process the user requests, this API forwards those requests to the Heat engine using the RPC.

heat-api-cfn

The heat-api-cfn module offers another API that is compatible with AWS CloudFormation. It also processes queries after forwarding them to heat-engine over RPC.

heat-engine

The heat-engine is the core component of the Orchestration service for OpenStack. It is responsible for launching new services and instances according to the given templates.

Heat Orchestration Template (HOT) specification

Heat Orchestration Template (HOT) is a new template format developed as an alternative to the **CloudFormation** template. The following specification explains the architecture of the HOT template format.

The following diagram depicts the logical architecture of the Heat module for OpenStack:

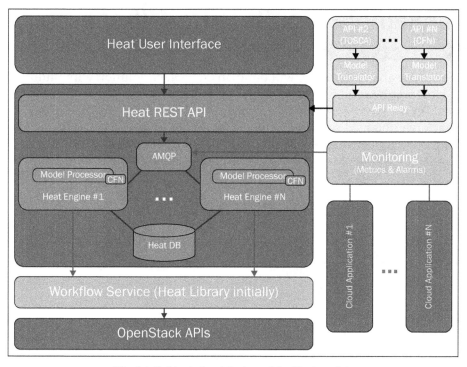

The detailed logical architecture of the Heat module

The following diagram shows how Heat components communicate with each other for a given user request for orchestration:

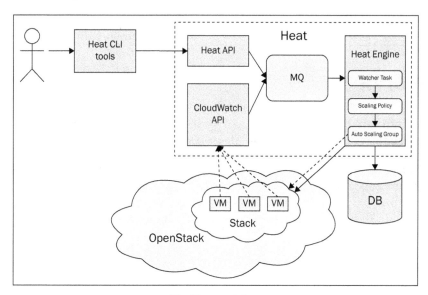

The Heat workflow

The example architecture 1 (based on the Nova network)

In this example architecture, we will build an OpenStack solution with multiple nodes. However, we will use the legacy networking features of OpenStack in this architecture. Another example architecture will follow that is built using the OpenStack neutron networking. In this example architecture, we have ensured to make the VMS high available so that in case one compute node goes down, the other will take its place while not affecting the virtual machines.

Node hardware specifications

Type	Example hardware
Controller	Model: Dell R620
	CPU: 2x Intel Xeon CPU E5-2620 0 @ 2.00 GHz
	Memory: 32 GB
	Disk: Two 300 GB 10000 RPM SAS disks
	Network: Two 10G network ports
Compute	Model: Dell R620
	CPU: 2x Intel Xeon CPU E5-2650 0 @ 2.00 GHz
	Memory: 128 GB
	Disk: Two 600 GB 10000 RPM SAS Disks
	Network: Four 10G network ports (for future proofing expansion)

An overview

An OpenStack cloud environment can be built using a single machine with a single NIC at a minimum; however, this can only be for educational or learning purposes and is not recommended for a large-scale or production environments.

In this example architecture, we are using a multinode OpenStack solution with more than one compute nodes for high availability. There can be multiple storage nodes, controller nodes, networking nodes as well, but for the sake of simplicity, we are building this system with single controller, block storage, and ephemeral storage nodes.

The following table shows the detailed specification for this example architecture:

Component	Details
OpenStack release	Juno
Host operating system	Ubuntu 14.04 LTS
OpenStack package repository	Ubuntu Cloud archive
Hypervisor	KVM
Database	MySQL
Message queue	RabbitMQ
Networking service	Nova-network
Network manager	FlatDHCP
Orchestration engine	Heat
Image service (glance) back end	File
Identity service (keystone) driver	SQL
Block storage service (cinder) back end	LVM/iSCSI
Live migration backend	Shared storage using NFS
Object storage	OpenStack object storage (Swift)

A detailed description

The detailed solution architecture is built using a cloud controller and several compute nodes running hypervisor and virtual machines.

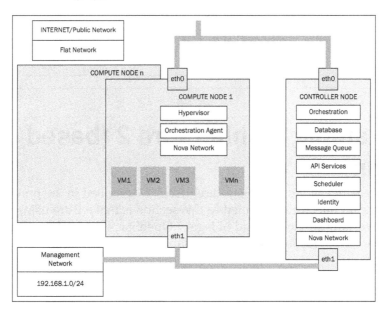

The controller node runs the Orchestration service (Heat), a block storage service for storing volumes, a network time protocol service, database service, API services, scheduler, identity service, image services (glance-api and glance-registry), and storage services.

The compute nodes run the hypervisor (in our case, it is KVM) and the necessary drivers for hypervisor. The compute nodes also facilitate live migration of instances from one node to another node.

As mentioned earlier, in this architecture, we are using the legacy networking for OpenStack and not the Neutron networking; therefore, we are incorporating all the networking services into the controller node and not installing a separate network node.

The network connectivity for a compute node n is described in the following diagram:

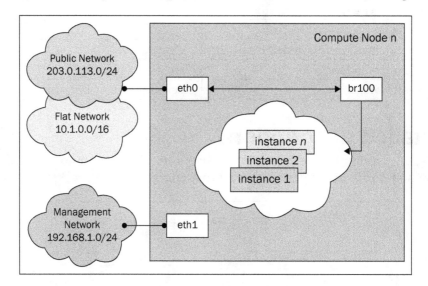

The example architecture 2 (based on Neutron)

The difference between the OpenStack architecture described in the previous section and the architecture explained in this section is that we are using the Neutron networking service instead of legacy OpenStack networking. Secondly, in this section, we are focusing on high availability of the solution.

Let's now take a look at the node hardware specifications for the basic architecture with OpenStack networking:

Type	Example hardware
Controller	Model: Dell R620
	CPU: 2x Intel Xeon CPU E5-2620 0 @ 2.00 GHz
	Memory: 32 GB
	Disk: Two 300 GB 10000 RPM SAS Disks
	Network: Two 10G network ports
Compute	Model: Dell R620
	CPU: 2x Intel Xeon CPU E5-2650 0 @ 2.00 GHz
	Memory: 128 GB
	Disk: Two 600 GB 10000 RPM SAS Disks
	Network: Four 10G network ports (for future proofing expansion)
Storage	Model: Dell R720xd
	CPU: 2x Intel Xeon CPU E5-2620 0 @ 2.00 GHz
	Memory: 64 GB
	Disk: Two 500 GB 7200 RPM SAS Disks and twenty-four 600 GB 10000 RPM SAS Disks
	Raid controller: PERC H710P integrated RAID controller, 1 GB NV Cache
	Network: Two 10G network ports
Network	Model: Dell R620
	CPU: 1x Intel Xeon CPU E5-2620 0 @ 2.00 GHz
	Memory: 32 GB
	Disk: Two 300 GB 10000 RPM SAS Disks
	Network: Five 10G network ports
Utility	Model: Dell R620
	CPU: 2x Intel Xeon CPU E5-2620 0 @ 2.00 GHz
	Memory: 32 GB
	Disk: Two 500 GB 7200 RPM SAS Disks
	Network: Two 10G network ports

Source: `http://docs.openstack.org/openstack-ops/content/example_architecture.html`

The following table shows the details of components used in this architecture:

Component	Details
OpenStack release	Juno
Host operating system	Red Hat Enterprise Linux 6.5, CentOS 6.5
OpenStack package repository	Red Hat Distributed OpenStack (RDO)
Hypervisor	KVM
Database	MySQL
Message queue	Qpid
Networking service	OpenStack networking
Tenant network separation	VLAN
Image service (Glance) backend	GlusterFS
Identity service (Keystone) driver	SQL
Block storage service (Cinder) backend	GlusterFS

Network layout for OpenStack networking

The network infrastructure includes all hardware devices involved in running the whole OpenStack solution, for example the switches, load balancers, servers, storage devices, and so on.

OpenStack uses several small network segments for establishing communication between different components. These network segments are described in the following sections.

The internal network

The internal network (as the name indicates) is used by the OpenStack components for communicating with each other for carrying out different functions, including provisioning of physical nodes, and communication between different node types using the OpenStack API.

The public network

The public network is used for accessing the Horizon interface of OpenStack and also for configuring floating IPs on the public facing interfaces of the virtual machine instances.

The OpenStack controller nodes are connected to this network so that the OpenStack Horizon interface can be accessed. It is also used to connect the VMs to the Internet, and therefore, the compute nodes are also part of this network.

The VM traffic network (private network)

The VM traffic network is only used by the compute nodes and networking nodes for internal communication related to virtual machine instances. It includes routing information being shared by the networking node and the floating IPs being assigned by the network node to the virtual machine instances on the compute node.

The physical connectivity of nodes

The following diagram shows how the different nodes are connected to each other using the network segments described earlier. It also includes the redundancy measures taken place to reduce the network outage due to faults.

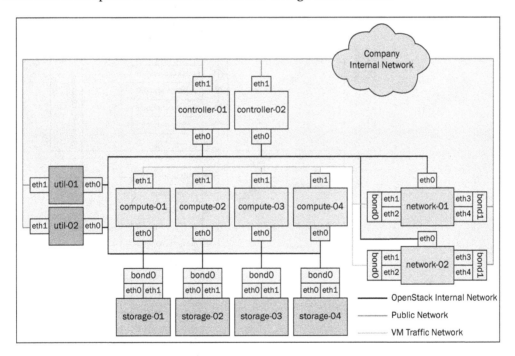

Individual node connectivity diagrams

The following diagrams depict the detailed connectivity of each node type to different network segments supported by OpenStack. These diagrams show the connectivity that is used to achieve availability and scalability:

Controller nodes

The cloud controller runs the dashboard, the API services, the database (MySQL), a message queue server (RabbitMQ), the scheduler for choosing compute resources (nova-scheduler), identity services (keystone, nova-consoleauth), image services (glance-api, glance-registry), services for console access of guests, and block storage services, including the scheduler for storage resources (cinder-api and cinder-scheduler):

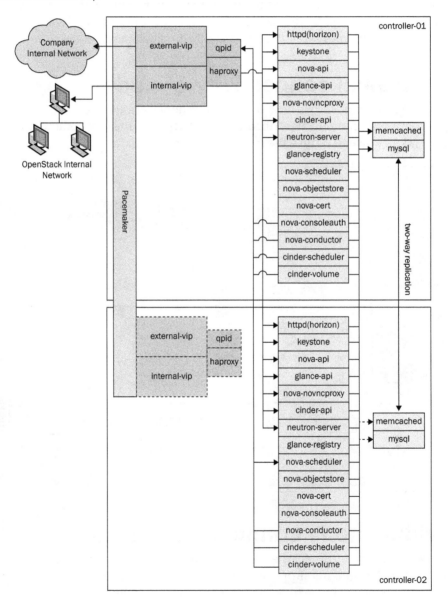

Compute nodes

The following diagram shows the connectivity of a compute node to the OpenStack networks, including the internal network and VM Traffic network:

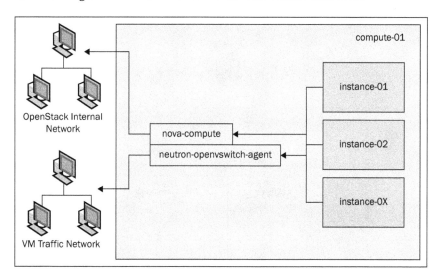

Network nodes

Using the OpenStack Neutron networking, separate nodes can be introduced for providing the networking features for the cloud system. The following diagram shows two networking nodes in a high available mode, using a pacemaker cluster. It shows the connectivity to different OpenStack network segments.

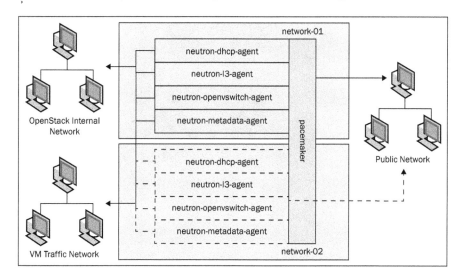

Storage nodes

The following diagram shows the connectivity of several storage nodes in a clustered environment using pacemaker and HA proxy:

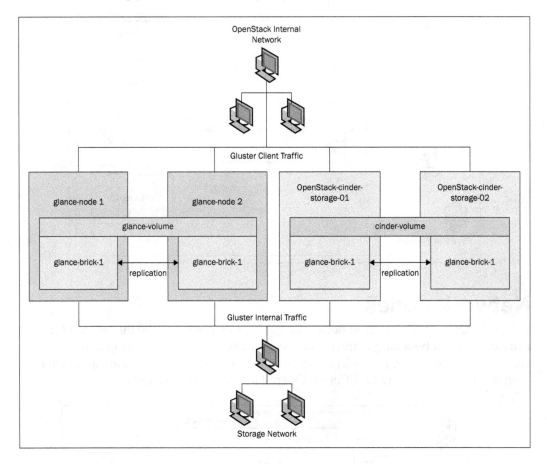

Summary

In this chapter, we learned about the detailed OpenStack architecture. Heat is an important component of OpenStack and provides orchestration services for deploying OpenStack services in an ordered manner. We discussed the OpenStack node types, including controller node, compute node, network node, storage node, and other utility nodes. We discussed that a simple OpenStack solution may contain a single physical machine with a single NIC at minimum; however, this can be useful for educational or testing purposes only. We also discussed that in a production environment, each of the OpenStack node types can be installed on a separate physical machine or even more than one machines. We also discussed a three-node OpenStack architecture composed of one controller/networking node and two compute nodes. In a later section of the chapter, we explained two example architectures. The first architecture used the legacy networking in OpenStack, which is also known as Nova networking. In the second architecture example, we explained the OpenStack Neutron networking component and the features such as VLANs provided by it. This chapter also described the conceptual and physical connectivity diagrams for the example architectures.

In the next chapter, we will discuss Heat stacks and templates. We will also cover the high availability features and autoscaling features supported by Heat. The next chapter will also cover nested stacks.

3
Stack Group of Connected Cloud Resources

In this chapter, we will study the basics of Heat stacks and templates. We will also discuss the autoscaling and high availability mechanisms supported by Heat.

The following are the learning objectives of this chapter:

- Heat basics: stacks and templates
- Autoscaling
- HA mechanism for the different levels (services running inside an instance, individual instances, stacks)
- Nested stacks

Please refer to `http://docs.openstack.org/developer/heat/glossary.html` for the explanations of all the terminologies used in the chapter.

Heat basics

Heat is a major project of OpenStack that is focused on orchestration and autoscaling. It allows deployment of complex cloud applications by defining them in text files, which it calls templates. The Heat engine parses and processes these templates. Heat understands the template format used by AWS CloudFormation, while there is a native Heat template format called **HOT**. The compatibility with AWS CloudFormation template system makes it possible to use several existing the AWS CloudFormation templates to be used with OpenStack.

A great advantage of orchestration is the ability of treating hardware infrastructure as code and providing features for autoscalability.

The source code for infrastructure can also be checked into version control as it can be done for software programs. Use of the YAML markup for templates makes this easy; therefore, HOT templates use YAML instead of JSON.

There are two types of APIs currently being supported by Heat; they are:

- The OpenStack native REST API
- The CloudFormation compatible Query API

Heat evolved as a counterpart to the AWS CloudFormation service; and therefore, it accepts the templates used in AWS and also provides a compatible API. The recent developments in OpenStack have provided additional features to orchestration service by introducing a native template format for OpenStack called **Heat Orchestration Template (HOT)**.

Stacks

Heat uses the stack to define a collection of resources combined together into a group for orchestration or scaling. These resources may include **virtual machine (VM)** instances, routers, switches, ports, router interfaces, security groups, subnets, storage volumes, and so on.

Templates

A template is a text file containing the definitions of resources, which are grouped into a stack. In other words, we can say that Heat uses templates to define stacks. For example, if there is a need to define a stack with two virtual machine instances connected to each other using a private network, then the template will be created by defining the two instances, a private network, a subnet, and two network ports. Heat supports the AWS CloudFormation template types as well as the **Heat Orchestration Template (HOT)** syntax.

CFN

CloudFormation is the template format devised by AWS and is also compatible with OpenStack Heat. The CFN-formatted templates are written in JSON rather that YAML as it is the case with HOT templates.

Heat Orchestration Template (HOT)

HOT is a new template format meant to replace the Heat **CloudFormation-compatible format** (**CFN**) as the native format supported by Heat over time. HOT templates are regular text files that are written using YAML.

The HOT system is still under continuous development and efforts are underway to support all the functionality that is currently available via the CFN compatible template interface. Currently HOT is not backward compatible with CFN, and can only be used with OpenStack Heat.

The HOT template example

Let's think of a very basic HOT template that consists of a single resource definition using the basic predefined properties. In this example, we want to deploy a single instance of a compute node:

```
heat_template_version: 2013-05-23
description: Template that deploys single compute node.
resources:
my_compute-01:
type: OS::Nova::Server
properties:
key_name: my_key
image: F18-x86_64-cfntools
flavor: m1.small
```

Let's explain the attributes of the previous example HOT template.

Heat_template_version

This is a mandatory attribute that is present in each HOT template. This describes the version of HOT template syntax. The value `2013-05-23` means it's the first version of the HOT template system. Currently, there are newer versions of HOT template syntax that are integrated with the later versions of OpenStack. The newer versions of templates can be downloaded from the link at `https://github.com/openstack/heat-templates`.

Description

The `description` attribute is an optional attribute that describes the template and its purpose.

Resources

The `resources` attribute is one of the most important sections of the HOT template. This lists the resources being controlled by the template and the type of resources. In this example, there is only a single resource mentioned and that is `my_comput-01`. The type of resource is `OS::Nova::Server`, which is the type of a compute node.

Properties or parameters

The properties subsection identifies the name of image, the flavor, and the keys being used for this compute resource.

Resource types

Heat uses more than 70 resource types that can be used in a stack created by Heat. The following are the most commonly used resource types in Heat templates:

- The Nova server (VM instance)
- Floating IP addresses
- Volumes (storage)
- Security groups
- Key pairs

Other resource types supported by Heat are listed as under:

- `OS::Barbican::Order`
- `OS::Barbican::Secret`
- `OS::Ceilometer::Alarm`
- `OS::Ceilometer::CombinationAlarm`
- `OS::Ceilometer::GnocchiAggregationByMetricsAlarm`
- `OS::Ceilometer::GnocchiAggregationByResourcesAlarm`
- `OS::Ceilometer::GnocchiResourcesAlarm`
- `OS::Cinder::Volume`
- `OS::Cinder::VolumeAttachment`
- `OS::Cinder::VolumeType`
- `OS::Glance::Image`
- `OS::Heat::AccessPolicy`
- `OS::Heat::AutoScalingGroup`

- `OS::Heat::CWLiteAlarm`
- `OS::Heat::CloudConfig`
- `OS::Heat::HARestarter`
- `OS::Heat::InstanceGroup`
- `OS::Heat::MultipartMime`
- `OS::Heat::RandomString`
- `OS::Heat::ResourceGroup`
- `OS::Heat::ScalingPolicy`
- `OS::Heat::SoftwareComponent`
- `OS::Heat::SoftwareConfig`
- `OS::Heat::SoftwareDeployment`
- `OS::Heat::SoftwareDeployments`
- `OS::Heat::Stack`
- `OS::Heat::StructuredConfig`
- `OS::Heat::StructuredDeployment`
- `OS::Heat::StructuredDeployments`
- `OS::Heat::SwiftSignal`
- `OS::Heat::SwiftSignalHandle`
- `OS::Heat::UpdateWaitConditionHandle`
- `OS::Heat::WaitCondition`
- `OS::Heat::WaitConditionHandle`
- `OS::Keystone::Group`
- `OS::Keystone::Project`
- `OS::Keystone::Role`
- `OS::Keystone::User`
- `OS::Neutron::ExtraRoute`
- `OS::Neutron::Firewall`
- `OS::Neutron::FirewallPolicy`
- `OS::Neutron::FirewallRule`
- `OS::Neutron::FloatingIP`
- `OS::Neutron::FloatingIPAssociation`
- `OS::Neutron::HealthMonitor`

- `OS::Neutron::IKEPolicy`
- `OS::Neutron::IPsecPolicy`
- `OS::Neutron::IPsecSiteConnection`
- `OS::Neutron::LoadBalancer`
- `OS::Neutron::MeteringLabel`
- `OS::Neutron::MeteringRule`
- `OS::Neutron::Net`
- `OS::Neutron::NetworkGateway`
- `OS::Neutron::Pool`
- `OS::Neutron::PoolMember`
- `OS::Neutron::Port`
- `OS::Neutron::ProviderNet`
- `OS::Neutron::Router`
- `OS::Neutron::RouterGateway`
- `OS::Neutron::RouterInterface`
- `OS::Neutron::SecurityGroup`
- `OS::Neutron::Subnet`
- `OS::Neutron::VPNService`
- `OS::Nova::Flavor`
- `OS::Nova::FloatingIP`
- `OS::Nova::FloatingIPAssociation`
- `OS::Nova::KeyPair`
- `OS::Nova::Server`
- `OS::Nova::ServerGroup`
- `OS::Sahara::Cluster`
- `OS::Sahara::ClusterTemplate`
- `OS::Sahara::NodeGroupTemplate`
- `OS::Swift::Container`
- `OS::Trove::Cluster`
- `OS::Trove::Instance`
- `OS::Zaqar::Queue`

Autoscaling

Autoscaling is a feature in cloud computing that allows computing resources to be added or removed from a computing group (also called a stack) dynamically. This modification of resources is made depending upon the load requirements of the stack. Automatic elasticity is another term used for autoscaling. Automatically growing or shrinking the computing power allows the datacenter resource optimization and cost savings.

Vertical scaling versus horizontal scaling

We will now seek to understand the basic differences between these two scaling methods.

Vertical scaling

Vertical scaling refers to adding more resources to a server or computing machine by adding more CPU, RAM, storage, and so on. Vertical scaling is also known as scale up. There are pros and cons of vertically scaling a computer which are mentioned in the following diagram:

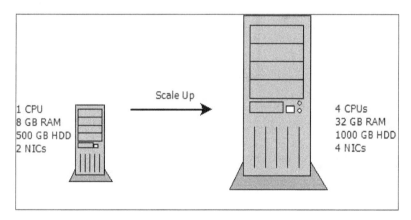

Let's discuss the pros and cons of vertical scaling:

Pros	Cons
• Vertical scaling will require less power consumption then running multiple servers • Cooling and environmental costs are less as compared to scale out • This is generally easier to implement and maintain • This requires less space and also footprints	• Price for such hardware is comparatively high as we need a server with the highest specs and options • Risk of outage is higher because of single point of failure • Vendor locked-in situation may occur because of limitations related to upgrading

Horizontal scaling

Horizontal scaling generally refers to adding more servers with not very high specifications and resources. The price for such hardware is comparatively less than the price for a server with highest specifications.

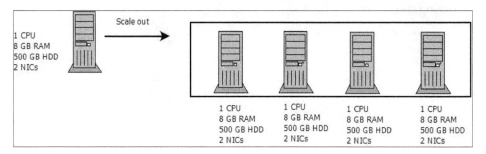

Let's discuss the pros and cons of horizontal scaling:

Pros	Cons
• The onetime cost in horizontal scaling is comparatively less than the cost involved in vertical scaling • It is easier to handle outages as more redundancy is available • Upgrading is still possible	• There is more space requirement and footprint in the data center • Higher operational costs, including power consumption and cooling • Additional cost may be involved for associated hardware including switches and routers

Autoscaling with Heat

Similar to AWS CloudFormation, Heat allows creating autoscaling of stacks and supports horizontal scaling (scale out). This is possible by monitoring the load and other performance metrics from the computing resources of the VM instances and then performing some actions when a performance metric, for example CPU load, crosses a given threshold. The action to be performed is usually to create another VM instance to share the burden on the overloaded VM instance.

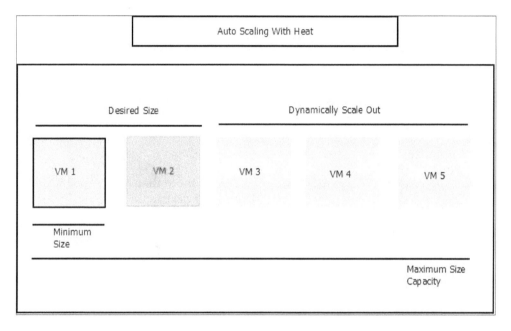

Heat in OpenStack provides such elasticity, which is normally not available in traditional virtualization environments. The **National Institute of Science and Technology (NIST)** defines this as an essential characteristics of cloud computing.

How autoscaling works in Heat

Heat supports horizontal autoscaling of compute nodes. The following are a few autoscaling principals for Heat:

- Autoscaling is initiated based on certain performance metrics
- Performance metrics may include CPU utilization, memory utilization, and others
- Heat supports HA load balancer controls and equally distributes load between the VM instances

- Heat agents are installed on individual VM instances that send periodic updates regarding the performance metrics to the Heat monitoring component
- It is the Heat monitoring component (CloudWatch) that is responsible for ensuring communication between the VMs and Heat
- The Heat engine provides the core functionality of autoscaling the VM instances

High availability

High availability refers to the maximum uptime of a server without service disruption or downtime. In network and datacenter terminology, high availability is measured relative to 100 percent operational or never crashing since its start. High availability ensures two important points:

- Minimize system downtime
- Minimize data loss

Downtime occurs when a service is not available for more than a specified time period. Data loss occurs due to accidental deletion or destruction of data.

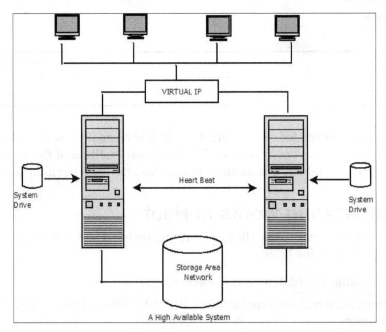

A High Available System

Many of the HA solutions ensure service guarantee only in scenarios of single entity failure; however, a robust high available system must provide service guarantee even in situations where multiple failures or cascading failures do occur.

High available systems mostly focus on addressing **single point of failures** (SPOFs). A single point of failure can be a device, cable, port, or any other resource that may cause service disruption and outage if it is not available due to any technical fault. Redundant resources are deployed to avoid SPOFs and achieve high availability.

These redundant resources may include the following:

- Network elements, including servers, switches, load balances, and routers
- Applications and software for automatic traffic shifting
- Redundant storage devices
- Cabling and connectivity devices
- Environmental arrangements

In case of failure of multiple independent devices, high available systems might fail too. However, the data must still be protected in such cases.

A nicely designed high available system typically provides uptimes of around 99.999 percent, which is roughly equivalent o less than an hour of cumulative downtime in 365 days. In these solutions, the recovery time is very short and is less than a few minutes.

OpenStack is designed while keeping in mind such types of high availability solutions. For its own infrastructure it supports high availability of more than 99.999 percent; however, this is not for the individual VM instances running inside OpenStack.

It is also very necessary to understand the nature of a service being stateful or stateless while designing high availability solutions.

Stateless versus stateful services

A stateless service does not require a series of user requests to work smoothly, but it provides a response to the user request and then no further action is required.

In order to design a high available solution for a stateless service redundant VM instances are required, which are connected behind a load balancer. The following OpenStack services are stateless:

- Nova-API
- Nova-Conductor
- Glance-API
- Keystone-API

- Neutron-API
- Nova-Scheduler
- Heat-API

Services that are stateful require a sequence of user requests to perform an action. They are comparatively difficult to maintain and manage as a single action requires more than one requests. Redundant instances behind a load balancer may not be sufficient to ensure high availability but additional steps need to be taken. These additional steps may vary depending upon the type of high availability design, which may fall into either of the following two categories:

- Active/Passive
- Active/Active

Active/Passive

Using this configuration, a high available system consists of redundant resources; however, one of the resources is active at a time and others are in HOT standby mode. If the active device fails due to some technical fault, the redundant devices become active and start serving the user requests.

If the service is a stateless service, then simply adding an active/passive device in the HA mode will do the job of high availability. However, if the service is a stateful service, then only adding an active/passive pair of redundant devices may not be sufficient. In this case, another application may be needed to synchronize the state of both active and passive devices.

As an example, we can say that the DNS server is a stateless service, which can be made high available by adding a redundant DNS server to the stack. In this case, one DNS server can be active, while the other can be in a HOT standby mode and resume operations when the first server is down. Both the DNS servers may listen to a single virtual IP address in this case.

Now, let's take an example of a stateful service in active/passive mode. A DHCP server, on the other hand, is a stateful service that keeps a history of the DHCP leases in a file. Now to make a high available solution in active/passive mode, we need to run an application such as Corosync to synchronize the latest DHCP leases file. In this case, if the active DHCP server dies due to a technical fault, the passive redundant DHCP instance will come up with the latest DHCP lease information because it was already synchronized with the old active server.

Active/Active

In an active/active mode, a high available solution has redundant nodes listening to user requests both at the same time. In this case, the high available redundant instances take equal load while still serving as a backup to each other. In this case, if one of the server instances dies, the other one will take the additional load and the users may not feel any service outage.

Let's consider our example of the DNS service, which we discussed earlier. In this case, we will be deploying the DNS server instances in the active/active mode. Both the DNS server instances will take the load and will serve to user requests. However, if any of the DNS instances goes down due to a technical fault, then the other instance will take the additional load of the faulty instance.

Now, let's consider the example of the stateful DHCP service in the active/active mode. In this case, both the instances will cater to user requests while sharing the single DHCP leases file or database.

The database will be kept up to date by both the instances and if any of the instances goes down then the other instance will take the additional load of the faulty instance while still using the latest DHCP leases file.

The discussed scenarios are some of the mostly used or common implementations for high available solutions but these are not the only ways to achieve high availability. The objective is to achieve high availability and it depends upon how we design our system and want it to behave in case of a network failure.

HA mechanisms for different levels

While using Heat in OpenStack, we are mostly interested in high availability mechanisms at three levels:

- HA for services running inside an instance
- HA for instances (virtual machine redundancy)
- HA for a logical group of instances (stack)

Fortunately, Heat supports all three levels of redundancy and high availability. It monitors all three levels and can perform an action in case of any service failure or network fault.

As an example, if Heat detects a failure in the database service, it can restart the database service. If the problem still persists after several restarts, the whole instance can be restarted and even if the problem still persists on the stack level then Heat can restart the whole stack of database servers.

Heat has yet another resource type called `AutoScalingGroup`, which, in many ways, is similar to `ResourceGroup`. The difference is that the `AutoScalingGroup` resource can be configured to apply scaling changes on certain events, triggered by Ceilometer or by a custom monitoring agent. With this resource, you can create scaling policy rules that alter the size of the server pool based on CPU usage or any other variable that can be monitored.

We have two viable options for autoscaling Heat stacks:

- Create cron jobs that send `stack-update` calls on a schedule (assuming it is possible to predict server loads).

- Install a custom monitoring script on an instance dedicated to that purpose. This instance can receive the list of servers as a property (like the `lib/haproxy.yaml` nested template does) and periodically SSH into the servers to take a look at the load or any other variable. This instance can then make a scaling up or down decision based on the readings obtained from the servers and send a `stack-update` call into Heat to make an adjustment.

Horizontal scaling and databases

Consider a MySQL server like the one you can start using a nested template. The instance that runs the MySQL server has its own storage, be it internal or external.

If we deploy several copies of the MySQL nested template, then we end up with several independent MySQL servers, each with its own separate storage. Pointing all the instances to the same storage does not really help much, because then the storage remains a bottleneck that puts a limit to how far out you can scale.

For the database scaling to work, you need all these independent storages to be synchronized, so that when a write operation happens on one of them, the operation is replicated on all the others. Database replication is a tough problem to solve, and not all database servers have a solution for it. For MySQL specifically, there are a few options. In my experience, the Galera Cluster is by far the best option. So, to have a horizontally scaled MySQL server, you would create another nested template that deploys Galera instead of plain MySQL. This nested template would export the same outputs as `lib/mysql.yaml`, so it can take its place on any templates that were made to work with the single-server database.

It is important to note that the issues with horizontal scaling are not exclusive of databases. In reality, any process that writes data to disk, even regular files, is potentially harder to scale due to the need to replicate writes to all the servers in the pool.

In the following sections, we will discuss two different approaches for HA mechanisms using Heat.

The approach – the metadata server and cfn-hup

The basic idea is to combine the CloudFormation instance metadata and the cfn-hup [1] to create a communication layer between the instance and Heat.

cfn-hup

cfn-hup is a script/daemon that runs inside the instance. It monitors the instance metadata and executes hooks when the metadata changes.

Currently, there are three triggers that cfn-hup provides hooks for:

*   post.add
*   post.update
*   post.remove

We would extend it to monitor the services specified in the AWS::CloudFormation::Init.services metadata and add a custom trigger (service.fail or something similar).

Heat's rescue/notification script would then hook into that and do its thing.

The metadata server

The metadata server stores the instance metadata and makes it available for reading and writing both from outside the instance and from within.

Heat would connect to the metadata server and get notified about service failures (and possibly other events). The Heat engine will decide whether there is a need to escalate and either restart the instance or the whole stack.

The notification will be done by polling at first. Later on, we'd probably switch to push.

For sending the events from the instances, we can extend the cfn-signal [2] script.

Benefits

The huge benefit of this approach is that we'd base it on tools and features that we need to build anyway for CloudFormation compatibility (metadata server, cfn-signal, cfn-hup).

Our extensions to these tools will not break compatibility and will be useful for needs other than HA.

Summary

Heat (the Orchestration service for OpenStack) uses template files to orchestrate resources and services for OpenStack. These template files are in fact text files that are created by the administrators. These templates support version control mechanisms.

Resources in a template file can be anything, including server instances, floating IP addresses, disk volumes, security policies or groups, and cloud users.

Heat along with the telemetry component (called Ceilometer) offers an autoscaling feature which is helpful in dynamic resource allocation.

The relationship between resources can also be specified in a template. For example, a disk volume can be associated with a server instance.

The entire life cycle of an instance or an application on an instance can be managed by Heat. A stack can be modified to make any changes in the cloud infrastructure. Heat will implement the modifications into the cloud after reading the newly updated template.

Heat was designed for effective management of the cloud infrastructure; however, the Heat templates are compatible with configuration management tools such as Chef and Puppet. A further development is in progress for improving the integration between software and infrastructure.

In the next chapter, we will install and configure an orchestration service and create, manage, and get information about stacks.

4

Installation and Configuration of the Orchestration Service

In this chapter, we will perform the actual installation of the OpenStack Orchestration service Heat. We will also write a simple template creating a stack. The following are the main objectives to be covered in this chapter:

- Orchestration module concepts
- Installing and configuring the Orchestration service
- Verifying the Orchestration service installation
- Creating and manage stacks
- Getting information about stacks
- Updating a stack

Orchestration module concepts

The Orchestration module is responsible for orchestrating cloud resources. As discussed in the earlier chapters, Heat is the Orchestration module for OpenStack. It manages resource types dynamically in an OpenStack environment. These resource types are defined in a template file. The template can be either in the AWS CloudFormation format or in the OpenStack HOT format. The resource types managed by OpenStack Heat could be any of the following:

- Compute instances
- Disk volumes
- Floating IP addresses
- Security groups
- Users
- Additional physical memory (RAM)

A few additional features provided by OpenStack Heat are:

- High availability
- Autoscaling
- Nested stacks

The following are the important components of Heat:

Name	Type	Description
Heat client	The command-line client	This is a command-line interface that interacts with the Heat API and runs orchestration commands using the AWS CloudFormation API.
heat-api	Component	This is an OpenStack-native REST API that processes API requests using RPC to the heat-engine.
heat-api-cfn	Component	This is a query API compatible with AWS CloudFormation. It is responsible for processing API requests by sending them to heat-engine over RPC.
heat-engine	Core	It is the core engine that orchestrates launching of templates and sends events back to the API consumer.

Installing and configuring Orchestration

Referring to the two scenarios discussed in *The example architecture 1 (based on the Nova network)* and *The example architecture 2 (based on Neutron)* sections of *Chapter 2, The OpenStack Architecture,* here are the architectural diagrams of both scenarios:

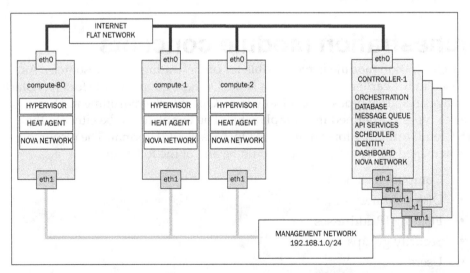

OpenStack Nova networking

The following image depicts the second scenario, which is based on OpenStack Neuron networking:

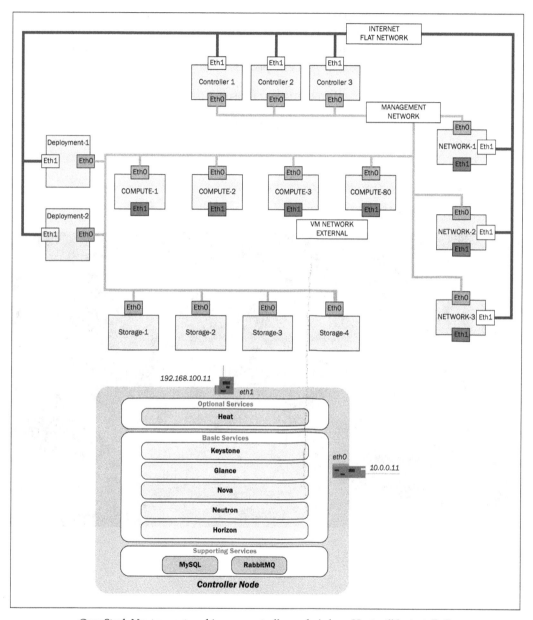

OpenStack Neutron networking—a controller node (where Heat will be installed)

This section describes how to install and configure the Orchestration module, code-named `heat`, on the controller node.

Assuming that all the core OpenStack services are installed as per the installation instructions available at OpenStack website, we will proceed towards installing the Heat component. Before installing and configuring Orchestration, we must create a database, service credentials, and API endpoints.

To create the database, we need to complete these steps:

1. Use the database access client to connect to the database server as the `root` user.

2. Create the `heat` database.

3. Grant proper access to the `heat` database.

4. Exit the database access client:

```
root@ubuntu:~# mysql -u root -p
Enter password:
Welcome to the MySQL monitor.  Commands end with ; or \g.
Your MySQL connection id is 50
Server version: 5.5.43-0ubuntu0.14.04.1 (Ubuntu)

Copyright (c) 2000, 2015, Oracle and/or its affiliates. All rights reserved.

Oracle is a registered trademark of Oracle Corporation and/or its
affiliates. Other names may be trademarks of their respective
owners.

Type 'help;' or '\h' for help. Type '\c' to clear the current input statement.

mysql> CREATE DATABASE heat;
Query OK, 1 row affected (0.00 sec)

mysql> GRANT ALL PRIVILEGES ON heat.* TO 'heat'@'localhost' IDENTIFIED BY 'openstack123';
Query OK, 0 rows affected (0.18 sec)

mysql> GRANT ALL PRIVILEGES ON heat.* TO 'heat'@'%' IDENTIFIED BY 'openstack123';
Query OK, 0 rows affected (0.00 sec)

mysql> quit;
Bye
```

5. Create a credentials file with the following command:

```
vi creds
```

The following variables should be exported:

```
ubuntu@ubuntu:~$ export SERVICE_TOKEN=openstack
ubuntu@ubuntu:~$ export OS_TENANT_NAME=admin
ubuntu@ubuntu:~$ export OS_USERNAME=admin
ubuntu@ubuntu:~$ export OS_PASSWORD=openstack
ubuntu@ubuntu:~$ export OS_AUTH_URL="http://localhost:5000/v2.0/"
ubuntu@ubuntu:~$ export SERVICE_ENDPOINT=http://localhost:35357/v2.0
```

6. Source the `admin` credentials to gain access to admin-only CLI commands:

```
$ source creds
```

7. To create the service credentials, complete these steps:

    1. Create the `heat` user.

    2. Add the `admin` role to the `heat` user.

    3. Create the `heat_stack_owner` role.

    4. Add the `heat_stack_owner` role to the demo `tenant` and `user`.

    5. Create the `heat_stack_user` role.

8. Create the `heat` and `heat-cfn` service entities:

```
root@ubuntu:~# keystone service-create --name heat --type orchestration --description "Openstack Orc
hestration Service"
+-------------+-----------------------------------+
|   Property  |               Value               |
+-------------+-----------------------------------+
| description |  Openstack Orchestration Service  |
|   enabled   |               True                |
|     id      |  0e43d4ac5bb54991a48fe023bc307dfd |
|    name     |               heat                |
|    type     |           orchestration           |
+-------------+-----------------------------------+
root@ubuntu:~# keystone service-create --name heat-cfn --type cloudformation --description "Openstac
k Orchestration Cloudformation Service"
+-------------+-----------------------------------------------+
|   Property  |                     Value                     |
+-------------+-----------------------------------------------+
| description |  Openstack Orchestration Cloudformation Service |
|   enabled   |                     True                      |
|     id      |        3e436c043f454bed97f4cd57d392015b       |
|    name     |                    heat-cfn                   |
|    type     |                 cloudformation                |
+-------------+-----------------------------------------------+
root@ubuntu:~#
```

The Orchestration service automatically assigns the `heat_stack_user` role to users that it creates during stack deployment. By default, this role restricts API operations. To avoid conflicts, do not add this role to users with the `heat_stack_owner` role.

9. Create the Orchestration service API endpoints:

```
keystone endpoint-create --service-id $(keystone service-
list | awk '/ cloudformation / {print $2}' --public http://
localhost:8000/v2/%\(tenant_id\)s --region regionOne
```

We will get the following output for this command:

```
root@ubuntu:~# keystone endpoint-create --service-id $(keystone service-list | awk '/ cloudformation
/ {print $2 }') --publicurl http://192.168.5.38:8000/v1/%\(tenant_id\)s --internalurl http://192.16
8.5.38:8000/v1/%\(tenant_id\)s  --adminurl http://192.168.5.38:8000/v1/%\(tenant_id\)s  --region reg
ionOne
+-------------+-------------------------------------------+
|   Property  |                   Value                   |
+-------------+-------------------------------------------+
|   adminurl  |  http://192.168.5.38:8000/v1/%(tenant_id)s |
|      id     |      b792c5057a6746c9a6bf635bc131bc2f     |
| internalurl |  http://192.168.5.38:8000/v1/%(tenant_id)s |
|  publicurl  |  http://192.168.5.38:8000/v1/%(tenant_id)s |
|    region   |                 regionOne                 |
|  service_id |      3e436c043f454bed97f4cd57d392015b     |
+-------------+-------------------------------------------+
root@ubuntu:~# _
```

Installing and configuring the Orchestration components

Next, we will proceed towards the installation of Orchestration packages. The following three packages are required in order to have a working orchestration component for OpenStack:

- `openstack-heat-api`
- `openstack-heat-engine`
- `openstack-heat-api-cfn`

Run the following command to install these packages:

```
yum install openstack-heat-api openstack-heat-engine  openstack-heat-api-cfn
```

Next, we need to configure the Orchestration engine according to our requirements:

1. Edit the `/etc/heat/heat.conf` file and complete the following actions:

```
$ vi /etc/heat/heat.conf
```

2. In the `[database]` section, configure the database access:

```
[database]

# Options defined in oslo.db
# The file name to use with SQLite. (string value)
#sqlite_db=oslo.sqlite
# If True, SQLite uses synchronous mode. (boolean value)
#sqlite_synchronous=true
# The back end to use for the database. (string value)
# Deprecated group/name - [DEFAULT]/db_backend
#backend=sqlalchemy
# The SQLAlchemy connection string to use to connect to the
# database. (string value)
# Deprecated group/name - [DEFAULT]/sql_connection
# Deprecated group/name - [DATABASE]/sql_connection
# Deprecated group/name - [sql]/connection
#connection=<None>
connection = mysql://heat:openstack123@192.168.5.38/heat
```

3. Replace openstack123 with the password you chose for the Orchestration database.

4. In the [DEFAULT] section, configure the RabbitMQ message broker access:

```
[DEFAULT]

rpc_backend = rabbit
rabbit_host = controller
rabbit_password = RABBIT_PASS
```

5. Replace RABBIT_PASS with the password you chose for the guest account in RabbitMQ.

6. In the [keystone_authtoken] and [ec2authtoken] sections, configure identity service access:

```
[keystone_authtoken]
auth_uri = http://controller:5000/v2.0
identity_uri = http://controller:35357
admin_tenant_name = service
admin_user = heat
admin_password = HEAT_PASS

[ec2authtoken]
auth_uri = http://controller:5000/v2.0
```

7. Replace HEAT_PASS with the password you chose for the heat user in the Identity service. In the [DEFAULT] section, configure the metadata and wait condition URLs:

```
[DEFAULT]
heat_metadata_server_url = http://controller:8000
heat_waitcondition_server_url =
http://controller:8000/v1/waitcondition
```

8. (Optional) To assist with troubleshooting, enable verbose logging in the [DEFAULT] section:

```
[DEFAULT]
verbose = True
```

9. Populate the Orchestration database:

```
root@ubuntu:~# su -s /bin/sh -c "heat-manage db_sync" heat
```

Finalize installation

At this point, we need to restart the Orchestration services so that the new changes in the configurations may take effect, as shown in the following screenshot:

```
root@ubuntu:~# service heat-api restart
heat-api stop/waiting
heat-api start/running, process 15414
root@ubuntu:~# service heat-api-cfn restart
heat-api-cfn stop/waiting
heat-api-cfn start/running, process 15442
root@ubuntu:~# service heat-engine restart
stop: Unknown instance:
heat-engine start/running, process 15469
root@ubuntu:~# _
```

Verify operations

This section describes how to verify operations of the Orchestration module (Heat):

1. Source the demo tenant credentials:

```
$ source demoopenrc.sh
```

The Orchestration module uses templates to describe stacks. In the following sections, we will describe how to create a stack using Heat.

2. Create a test template in the `teststack.yml` file with the following content:

```
heat_template_version: 2013-05-23
description: Simple template to deploy a single compute instance
parameters:
 key_name:
   type: string
   label: Key Name
   description: Name of key-pair to be used for compute instance
 image_id:
   type: string
   label: Image ID
   description: Image to be used for compute instance
 instance_type:
   type: string
   label: Instance Type
   description: Type of instance (flavor) to be used
resources:
 my_instance:
   type: OS::Nova::Server
   properties:
     key_name: { get_param: key_name }
     image: { get_param: image_id }
     flavor: { get_param: instance_type }
```

3. Use the `heat stack-create` command to create a stack from the template:

```
$ NET_ID=$(nova net-list|awk '/demonet/{print $2}')
$ heat stack-create -f teststack.yml \
-P "ImageID=cirros0.3.3x86_64;NetID=$NET_ID" testStack
```

4. Use the `heat stack-list` command to verify the successful creation of the stack:

```
$ heat stack-list
```

5. Finally, the Orchestration option should be visible in OpenStack Heat:

OpenStack Heat installation

In this section, we will describe the steps for installing Heat on Ubuntu Linux:

1. Change to the super user mode:

```
$ sudo su
```

2. Install Heat packages:

```
root:~# apt-get install heat-api heat-api-cfn heat-engine

heat-engine start/running, process 4950
Setting up python-testtools (0.9.35-0ubuntu1) ...
Setting up python-fixtures (0.3.14-1ubuntu2) ...
Processing triggers for libc-bin (2.19-0ubuntu6.5) ...
Processing triggers for ureadahead (0.100.0-16) ...
```

3. Create a MySQL database for Heat:

```
Ubuntu@ubuntu:~$ mysql -u root -p
```

The default connection string to `sqlite_db` needs to be replaced with a new string to the MySQL database. The `HEAT_DBPASS` parameter needs to be replaced with the actual password for the `heat` database:

```
CREATE DATABASE heat;
GRANT ALL PRIVILEGES ON heat.* TO 'heat'@'localhost'
IDENTIFIED BY 'HEAT_DBPASS';
GRANT ALL PRIVILEGES ON heat.* TO 'heat'@'%' IDENTIFIED BY
'HEAT_DBPASS';
exit;
```

4. Configure the service user and role:

```
source creds
keystone user-create --name heat --pass --service-pass --email
heat@domain.com
keystone user-role-add --user heat --tenant service --role
admin
```

5. Register the service and create the endpoint:

```
ubuntu@ubuntu:~$ keystone service-create --name heat --type orchestration
--description "orchestration"
ubuntu@ubuntu:~$ Keystone endpoint-create \
--service-id=$(keystone service-list awk '/ orchestration / {print $2}') \
--publicurl=http://192.168.100.11:8004/v1/%\(tenant_id\)s \
--internalurl=http://controller:8004/v1/%\(tenant_id\)s \
--adminurl=http://controller:8004/v1/%\(tenant_id\)s

ubuntu@ubuntu:~$ keystone service-create --name heat-cfn --type cloudforma
tion --description "orchestration cloud formation"
ubuntu@ubuntu:~$ keystone endpoint-create \
--serviceid $(keystone service-list awk '/ cloudformation / {print $2}') \
--publicurl=http://192.168.100.11:8000/v1 \
--internalurl=http://controller:8000/v1 \
--adminurl=http://controller:8000/v1
```

6. Create the `heat_stack_user` role:

```
$ keystone role-create --name heat_stack_user
```

7. Install the OpenStack client:

```
$ apt-get install -y python-openstack-client
```

8. Create the `heat_stack_owner` role and give role to users (`admin` and `demo`) who create Heat stacks:

```
$ keystone-role-create --name heat-stack-owner

$ keystone user-role-add --user demo --tenant demo --role --
heat_stack_owner

$ keystone user-role-add --user admin --tenant demo --role
heat_stack_owner

$ keystone user-role-add --user admin --tenant admin --role
heat_stack_owner
```

9. Edit the `/etc/heat/heat.conf` file:

```
root: ~
root:~# vi /etc/heat/heat.conf
```

10. Replace the connection string, as shown in the following screenshot:

```
root: ~
#

# The backend to use for db (string value)
# Deprecated group/name - [DEFAULT]/db_backend
#backend=sqlalchemy


#
# Options defined in heat.openstack.common.db.sqlalchemy.session
#

# The SQLAlchemy connection string used to connect to the
# database (string value)
# Deprecated group/name - [DEFAULT]/sql_connection
# Deprecated group/name - [DATABASE]/sql_connection
# Deprecated group/name - [sql]/connection
# connection=sqlite:////var/lib/heat/$sqlite_db
connection=mysql://heat:heat_dbpass@controller_host/heat
# The SQLAlchemy connection string used to connect to the
# slave database (string value)
#slave_connection=

# timeout before idle sql connections are reaped (integer
```

After incorporating the changes, the configuration file `heat.conf` should look like the following screenshot:

```
[DEFAULT]
verbose = True
log_dir=/var/log/heat
rabbit_host = controller
heat_metadata_server_url = http://10.0.0.11:8000
heat_waitcondition_server_url =
http://10.0.0.11:8000/v1/waitcondition
# replace $HEAT_DOMAIN_ID variable by the id of heat domain
stack_user_domain=$HEAT_DOMAIN_ID
stack_domain_admin=heat_domain_admin
stack_domain_admin_password=service_pass
deferred_auth_method=trusts

[keystone_authtoken]
auth_host = controller
auth_port = 35357
auth_protocol = http
auth_uri = http://controller:5000/v2.0
admin_tenant_name = service
admin_user = heat
admin_password = service_pass

[ec2authtoken]
auth_uri = http://controller:5000/v2.0
```

It is also important to mention the `heat` instance user in the same configuration file under the [DEFAULT] section. `user_instance` is required to access VM via SSH. Heat will use the default user `ec2user` to configure user instance. This is also shown in the following screenshot:

```
⊗ ⊖ ⊡   root: ~
[DEFAULT]
#
# Options defined in heat.api.middleware.ssl
#
# original request protocol scheme was, even if it was removed
# by an SSL terminator proxy. (string value)
#secure_proxy_ssl_header=X-Forwarded-Proto


#
# Options defined in heat.common.config
#

# The default user for new instances. This option is
# deprecated and will be removed in the Juno release. If it's
# empty, Heat will use the default user set up with your cloud
# image (for OS::Nova::Server) or 'ec2-user' (for
# AWS::EC2::Instance). (string value)
#instance_user=ec2-user
instance_user=heat

# Driver to use for controlling instances. (string value)
#instance_driver=heat.engine.nova
```

11. Finally, we need to remove the default Heat SQLite database as we are using
    the MySQL database instead. This is just to make sure that we do not use it
    accidently. We can do it using the following command:

```
⊗ ⊖ ⊡   root: ~
root:~# rm -rf /var/lib/heat/heat.sqlite
root:~#
```

12. The next step is to synchronize the database:

```
⊗ ⊖ ⊡   root: ~
root:~# heat-manage db_sync
```

13. We need to restart the services using the following commands:

```
$ service heat-api start

$ service heat-api-cfn start

$ service heat-engine start
```

14. Finally, verify the operations while using the following commands:

```
$ source creds

$ heat stack-list
```

Creating a stack with Heat

Now that we have installed and configured the orchestration service for OpenStack, we need to use it, and this is the time to create a stack and see Heat in action. We will use the HOT template to define a stack. HOT is an OpenStack native template system that describes the resources, which will be managed by Heat. The following is the structure of a very basic HOT template:

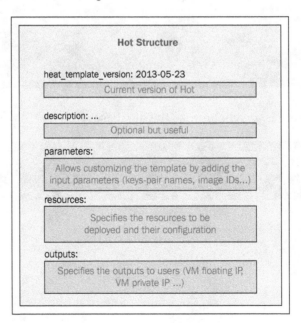

The following is an example of a working HOT template:

```
heat_template_version: 20130523

description: Hot Template to deploy a single server

parameters:
ImageID:
type: string
description: Image ID
NetID:
type: string
description: External Network ID

resources:
  server_0:
type: OS::Nova::Server
properties:
name: "server0"
image: { get_param: ImageID }
flavor: "m1.small"
networks:
network: { get_param: NetID }

outputs:
  server0_ip:
description: IP of the server
value: { get_attr: [ server_0, first_address ] }
```

Creating an advanced template for Heat

In this example, we will use two interconnected VMs with floating IP addresses accessible from the Internet:

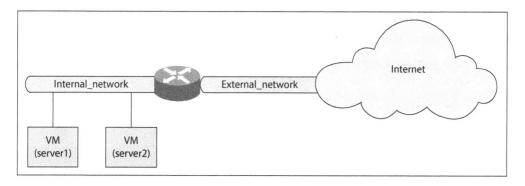

To deploy this stack, we need to specify different resources in the HOT template. The following diagram describes clearly resources and their dependencies:

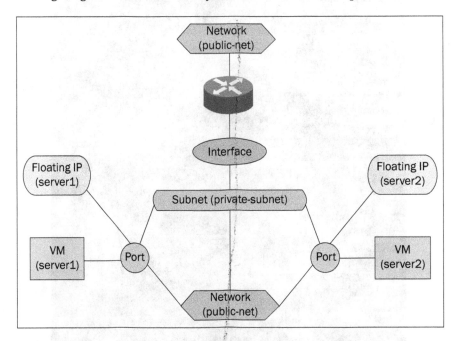

Let's describe the resources and their dependencies:

- The first resource we define is a private network (of type OS::Neutron::Net) to which we associate a resource of type subnet (OS::Neutron::Subnet).

- Second, we define a router (of type OS::Neutron::Router). We connect it to the preexisting public network (see properties section), and we connect it also to the private subnet by defining a router interface (of type OS::Neutron::RouterInterface).

- Then, for each defined server (OS::Nova::Server), we link it to a Neutron port resource (of type OS::Neutron::Port) and to a floating IP resource (of type OS::Neutron::FloatingIP).

- Each port represents a logical switch port and is linked to the default security group to insure secure access to VMs.

The floating IP addresses provide external (Internet) access to instances.

After identifying the needed resources, let's create template in the `firststack.yml` file with the following command:

```
$ vi firststack.yml
```

And the output looks like this:

```
heat_template_version: 20130523
description: HOT template for two interconnected VMs with floating ips.
parameters:
image_id:
type: string
description: Image Name
secgroup_id:
type: string
description : Id of the security group
public_net:
type: string
description: public network id
resources:
private_net:
type: OS::Neutron::Net
properties:
name: privatenet
private_subnet:
type: OS::Neutron::Subnet
properties:
network_id: { get_resource: private_net }
cidr: 172.16.2.0/24
gateway_ip: 172.16.2.1
  router1:
type: OS::Neutron::Router
properties:
external_gateway_info:
network: { get_param: public_net }
  router1_interface:
type: OS::Neutron::RouterInterface
properties:
router_id: { get_resource: router1 }
subnet_id: { get_resource: private_subnet }
  server1_port:
type: OS::Neutron::Port
properties:
network_id: { get_resource: private_net }
```

```
security_groups: [ get_param: secgroup_id ]
fixed_ips:
subnet_id: { get_resource: private_subnet }
  server1_floating_ip:
type: OS::Neutron::FloatingIP
properties:
floating_network_id: { get_param: public_net }
port_id: { get_resource: server1_port }
  server1:
type: OS::Nova::Server
properties:
name: Server1
image: { get_param: image_id }
flavor: m1.tiny
networks:
port: { get_resource: server1_port }
  server2_port:
type: OS::Neutron::Port
properties:
network_id: { get_resource: private_net }
security_groups: [ get_param: secgroup_id ]
fixed_ips:
subnet_id: { get_resource: private_subnet }
  server2_floating_ip:
type: OS::Neutron::FloatingIP
properties:
floating_network_id: { get_param: public_net }
port_id: { get_resource: server2_port }
  server2:
type: OS::Nova::Server
properties:
name: Server2
```

Creating a stack

Now that we have created our credentials file, we are good to go with creating a template file and create a stack. We will name our template as `firststack.yml`:

```
$ source creds
$ heat stack-create -f teststack.yml \
-P "ImageID=cirros0.3.3x86_64; NetID=$NET_ID" testStack
$ sec_id=$(nova secgroup-list | awk '/ default / { print $2 }')

$ heatstack-create -f firststack.yml \
-p image_id=cirros0.3.2x86_64 \
-p public_net=$net_id \
-p secgroup_id=$sec_id first_stack
```

Verifying a stack

Verify that the stack was created successfully:

```
$ heat stack-list
```

Here is a snapshot of the Horizon dashboard interface after stack launching:

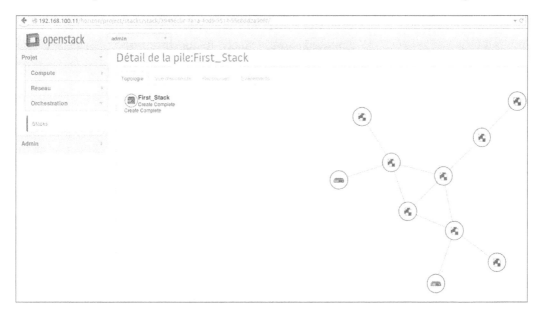

If you want to update a parameter of your stack (`secgroup_id`, `public_net`...),
run this command:

```
heat stack-update first-Stack -f firststack.yaml -P
PARAMETER_NAME=PARAMETER_NEW_VALUE
```

If you want to update your stack from a modified template file, run the command as
shown in the following screenshot:

```
NET_ID=$(nova net-list | awk '/ extnet / { print $2 }')

SEC_ID=$(nova sec-group-list | awk '/ default / { print $2 }')

heat stack-update First_Stack -f modifiedfirststack.yml \
-P image_id=cirros0.3.2x86_64 \
-P public_net=$NET_ID \
-P secgroup_id=$SEC_ID
```

Summary

In this document, we explained the steps required to install Heat on CentOS as well
as Ubuntu Linux. Although the syntax is slightly different for each distribution, the
overall process is similar. We created sample stacks using different scenarios.

In the next chapter, we will use more features of the orchestration service. We will
also use the basic commands provided by Heat CLI. The scaling features of Heat,
its roadmap, and architecture will be further discussed in the following chapters.

5
Working with Heat

In the previous chapter, we walked through installing and setting up Heat component for OpenStack. We created a very basic Heat template, and then we set up a simple stack using that template.

In this chapter, we will explore the architecture of Heat in further detail. We will focus on the following topics in this chapter:

- Standards used in Heat
- The Heat overview and roadmap
- The Heat basic architecture and CLI
- The Heat basic workflow
- The Heat API
- The Heat CloudWatch API
- The Heat engine
- Heat autoscaling principles
- JeOS

Standards used in Heat

The OpenStack Heat component complies to the following two standards:

- Amazon CloudFormation
- TOSCA

Amazon CloudFormation

AWS CloudFormation is an orchestration service introduced by Amazon, which enables users to define the cloud resources in a file called **template**. These resources are provisioned and configured by the provisioning engine automatically. All the dependencies are automatically solved by the provisioning engine itself.

The following are a few features offered by CloudFormation:

Simplified infrastructure management

A CloudFormation template simplifies infrastructure management by defining all the resources and their relationships into a single template file, and then building a stack using this template file. It reduces the time and effort required to install and then configure each service manually. This enables both the automated and unattended installation of services.

A quick replication of services

It is possible to configure services in a highly available mode using CloudFormation templates. Such services can be defined in multiple geographic locations or regions. In this case, if a service in one region becomes unavailable, then the users can access it from another region while noticing no downtime. This requires that these services are defined in more than one geographic region.

The template defining the resources and their relationships can be reused and applied in more than one region. This reduces the administrative effort for service provisioning and setup.

Track changes and control

The resources and relationships are stored in template files; therefore, any modifications to these template files can be easily identifying the differentiation between the original file and the modified file. This helps in rolling back any provisioning or configuration tasks performed for autoscaling purposes.

The TOSCA standard

Topology and Orchestration Specification for Cloud Applications (TOSCA) is a working group to standardize the orchestration of cloud applications. It works on portability and interoperability of cloud applications while being independent of the vendor who supplied this application.

The OpenStack Heat component was designed in such a way that it complies with the standards of TOSCA. Both CFN and HOT comply with this standard.

A topology template consists of a set of node templates and relationship templates that together define the topology model of a service as a (not necessarily connected) directed graph.

The following diagram describes the structural elements of a service template and their relationships:

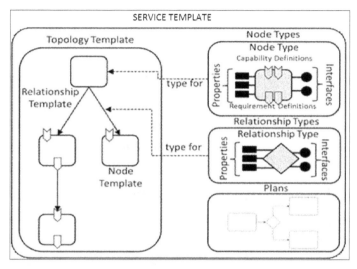

Source: http://docs.oasis-open.org/tosca/TOSCA/v1.0/os/TOSCA-v1.0-os.html

Heat overview and roadmap

The following is the detailed overview of the functionality provided by Heat to the other components of OpenStack:

- Heat uses templates: A text-based template file is used to describe the infrastructure of the cloud platform. This file is easily readable and can also be checked into version control.

- Resources are defined in a template: These are the building blocks of the cloud platform which include servers, floating IP addresses, disk volumes, users, security groups, and other types.

- Heat supports the autoscaling of servers and applications: The OpenStack Ceilometer component is used with Heat component to achieve autoscaling of virtual machine instances as well as applications running on top of them.

- Heat templates include relationships between resource types: A relationship is specified between different types of resources inside a Heat template. Heat uses these relationships to associate them with each other. A typical example of this can be a disk volume attached to a virtual machine instance. It helps Heat to call the OpenStack API in the right order and launch an application in the complete form.

- Heat can understand the complete lifecycle of an application. If we wanted to offload an application or a server instance, Heat will perform all those tasks in the right order.

- Heat integrates well with the configuration management tools such as Chef and Puppet. Heat was primarily designed to manage infrastructure based resources; however, the Heat templates can also be used to integrate with configuration management tools such as Chef, Puppet, and so on. Further developments in this regard are in progress.

The Heat architecture and CLI

The Heat project of OpenStack consists of several components, which interact with each other to provide the Orchestration service.

The following diagram depicts the high-level architecture of Heat components for OpenStack:

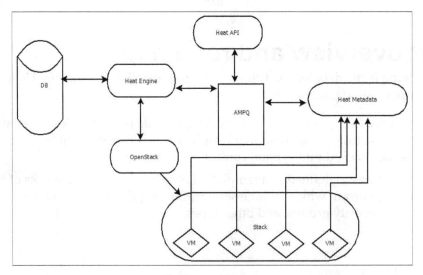

The Heat architecture

We will repeat the same table from *Chapter 4, Installation and Configuration of the Orchestration Service*, which includes the important components of Heat:

Name	Type	Description
Heat	The command-line client	There is a command-line interface that interacts with the Heat API and runs Orchestration commands using the AWS CloudFormation API.
heat-api	Component	This is an OpenStack-native REST API that processes API requests using RPC to the heat-engine.
heat-api-cfn	Component	This is a query API compatible with AWS CloudFormation. It is responsible for processing API requests by sending them to heat-engine over RPC.
heat-engine	Core	This is the core engine that orchestrates launching of templates and sends events back to the API consumer.

The Heat command-line reference

We will briefly discuss the command-line interface for Heat, which is used to interact with the Heat API.

Usage

Heat can accept almost 22 command-line arguments. We can display the default usage method by typing the following command with a wrong parameter (although this gives an error, but it displays the correct usage method):

```
ubuntu@ubuntu:~$ heat --usage
usage: heat [--version] [-d] [-v] [-k] [--os-cacert <ca-certificate>]
            [--cert-file CERT_FILE] [--key-file KEY_FILE] [--ca-file CA_FILE]
            [--api-timeout API_TIMEOUT] [--os-username OS_USERNAME]
            [--os-password OS_PASSWORD] [--os-tenant-id OS_TENANT_ID]
            [--os-tenant-name OS_TENANT_NAME] [--os-auth-url OS_AUTH_URL]
            [--os-region-name OS_REGION_NAME] [--os-auth-token OS_AUTH_TOKEN]
            [--os-no-client-auth] [--heat-url HEAT_URL]
            [--heat-api-version HEAT_API_VERSION]
            [--os-service-type OS_SERVICE_TYPE]
            [--os-endpoint-type OS_ENDPOINT_TYPE] [--include-password]
            <subcommand> ...
heat: error: too few arguments
ubuntu@ubuntu:~$
```

Getting help

A detailed help screen can be displayed by running the following command:

`ubuntu@openstackheat:~$heat  -- help | less`

After this, we'll get the output shown in the following screenshot:

```
usage: heat [--version] [-d] [-v] [-k] [--os-cacert <ca-certificate>]
            [--cert-file CERT_FILE] [--key-file KEY_FILE] [--ca-file CA
            [--api-timeout API_TIMEOUT] [--os-username OS_USERNAME]
            [--os-password OS_PASSWORD] [--os-tenant-id OS_TENANT_ID]
            [--os-tenant-name OS_TENANT_NAME] [--os-auth-url OS_AUTH_URL
            [--os-region-name OS_REGION_NAME] [--os-auth-token OS_AUTH_
            [--os-no-client-auth] [--heat-url HEAT_URL]
            [--heat-api-version HEAT_API_VERSION]
            [--os-service-type OS_SERVICE_TYPE]
            [--os-endpoint-type OS_ENDPOINT_TYPE] [--include-password]
            <subcommand> ...

Command-line interface to the Heat API.

Positional arguments:
  <subcommand>
    action-resume      Resume the stack.
    action-suspend     Suspend the stack.
    build-info         Retrieve build information.
    create             DEPRECATED! Use stack-create instead.
    delete             DEPRECATED! Use stack-delete instead.
    describe           DEPRECATED! Use stack-show instead.
    event              DEPRECATED! Use event-show instead.
    event-list         List events for a stack.
    event-show         Describe the event.
    gettemplate        DEPRECATED! Use template-show instead.
    list               DEPRECATED! Use stack-list instead.
    output-list        Show available outputs.
    output-show        Show a specific stack output.
    resource           DEPRECATED! Use resource-show instead.
    resource-list      Show list of resources belonging to a stack.
    resource-metadata  List resource metadata.
    resource-show      Describe the resource.
    resource-signal    Send a signal to a resource.
    resource-template  Generate a template based on a resource.
    resource-type-list List the available resource types.
:_
```

To see the next screen, we need to press the *Enter* key:

```
          resource-type-show  Show the resource type.
          stack-abandon       Abandon the stack.
          stack-adopt         Adopt a stack.
          stack-create        Create the stack.
          stack-delete        Delete the stack(s).
          stack-list          List the user's stacks.
          stack-preview       Preview the stack.
          stack-show          Describe the stack.
          stack-update        Update the stack.
          template-show       Get the template for the specified stack.
          template-validate   Validate a template with parameters.
          update              DEPRECATED! Use stack-update instead.
          validate            DEPRECATED! Use template-validate instead.
          bash-completion     Prints all of the commands and options to stdout.
          help                Display help about this program or one of its
                              subcommands.

Optional arguments:
  --version               Shows the client version and exits.
  -d, --debug             Defaults to env[HEATCLIENT_DEBUG].
  -v, --verbose           Print more verbose output.
  -k, --insecure          Explicitly allow the client to perform "insecure" SSL
                          (https) requests. The server's certificate will not be
                          verified against any certificate authorities. This
                          option should be used with caution.
  --os-cacert <ca-certificate>
                          Specify a CA bundle file to use in verifying a TLS
                          (https) server certificate. Defaults to env[OS_CACERT]
  --cert-file CERT_FILE
                          Path of certificate file to use in SSL connection.
                          This file can optionally be prepended with the private
                          key.
  --key-file KEY_FILE     Path of client key to use in SSL connection.This
                          option is not necessary if your key is prepended to
                          your cert file.
  --ca-file CA_FILE       Path of CA SSL certificate(s) used to verify the
:_
```

To see yet another screen, we need to press the *Enter* key one more time:

```
                         key.
--key-file KEY_FILE      Path of client key to use in SSL connection.This
                         option is not necessary if your key is prepended to
                         your cert file.
--ca-file CA_FILE        Path of CA SSL certificate(s) used to verify the
                         remote server's certificate. Without this option the
                         client looks for the default system CA certificates.
--api-timeout API_TIMEOUT
                         Number of seconds to wait for an API response,
                         defaults to system socket timeout
--os-username OS_USERNAME
                         Defaults to env[OS_USERNAME].
--os-password OS_PASSWORD
                         Defaults to env[OS_PASSWORD].
--os-tenant-id OS_TENANT_ID
                         Defaults to env[OS_TENANT_ID].
--os-tenant-name OS_TENANT_NAME
                         Defaults to env[OS_TENANT_NAME].
--os-auth-url OS_AUTH_URL
                         Defaults to env[OS_AUTH_URL].
--os-region-name OS_REGION_NAME
                         Defaults to env[OS_REGION_NAME].
--os-auth-token OS_AUTH_TOKEN
                         Defaults to env[OS_AUTH_TOKEN].
--os-no-client-auth      Do not contact keystone for a token. Defaults to
                         env[OS_NO_CLIENT_AUTH].
--heat-url HEAT_URL      Defaults to env[HEAT_URL].
--heat-api-version HEAT_API_VERSION
                         Defaults to env[HEAT_API_VERSION] or 1.
--os-service-type OS_SERVICE_TYPE
                         Defaults to env[OS_SERVICE_TYPE].
--os-endpoint-type OS_ENDPOINT_TYPE
                         Defaults to env[OS_ENDPOINT_TYPE].
--include-password       Send os-username and os-password to heat.

See "heat help COMMAND" for help on a specific command.
(END)
```

And finally, to quit this screen, we need to press : *and* Q keys.

Heat subcommands

The following table shows the subcommands supported by Heat:

Command	Description
action-check	This subcommand is used to check the state of a stack resource
action-resume	This subcommand is used to resume a suspended stack
action-suspend	This subcommand is used to suspend a stack
build-info	This subcommand is used to retrieve the build info or state of a stack
config-create	This subcommand is used to create software configuration

Command	Description
`config-delete`	This subcommand is used to delete a software configuration, which was already made by `config-create`
`config-show`	This subcommand is used to view details of software configuration
`deployment-create`	This subcommand is used to create a software deployment
`deployment-delete`	This subcommand is used to delete software deployments
`deployment-metadata-show`	This subcommand is used to get deployment configuration metadata for the specified server
`deployment-show`	This subcommand is used to show the details of a software deployment
`deployment-output-show`	This subcommand is used to display a stack output.
`event`	This subcommand is now deprecated; we can use event-show instead
`event-list`	This subcommand is used to list events for a stack
`event-show`	This subcommand is used to describe details of an event
`hook-clear`	This subcommand is used to clear hooks for a specific stack
`output-list`	This subcommand is used to display the available outputs
`output-show`	This subcommand is used to show a specific stack output
`resource-list`	This subcommand is used to display available resources in a stack
`resource-metadata`	This subcommand is used to list the resource metadata
`resource-show`	This subcommand is used to describe the resource
`help`	This subcommand is used to display help about this program or one of its subcommands
`resource-signal`	This subcommand is used send a signal to a resource
`resource-template`	This subcommand is deprecated; use resource-type-template instead
`resource-type-list`	This subcommand is used to list the available resource types
`resource-type-show`	This subcommand is used to show the resource type
`resource-type-template`	This subcommand is used to generate a template based on a resource type
`service-list`	This subcommand is used to list the Heat engines
`snapshot-delete`	This subcommand is used to delete a snapshot of a stack
`snapshot-list`	This subcommand is used to list the snapshots of a stack
`snapshot-show`	This subcommand is used to show a snapshot of a stack
`stack-abandon`	This subcommand is used to abandon the stack

Command	Description
`stack-adopt`	This sub command is used to adopt a stack
`stack-cancel-update`	This subcommand is used to cancel currently running update of the stack
`stack-create`	This subcommand is used to create the stack
`stack-delete`	This subcommand is used to delete the stack(s)
`stack-list`	This subcommand is used to list the user's stacks
`stack-preview`	This subcommand is used to preview the stack
`stack-restore`	This subcommand is used to restore a snapshot of a stack
`stack-show`	This subcommand is used to describe the stack
`stack-snapshot`	This subcommand is used to make a snapshot of a stack
`stack-update`	This subcommand is used to update the stack
`template-show`	This subcommand is used to get the template for the specified stack
`bash-completion`	This subcommand is used to print all of the commands and options to `stdout`
`template-validate`	This subcommand is used to validate a template with parameters

Heat optional arguments

A few arguments can be passed to the command-line based on the requirement. These are as follows:

- `--version`: This shows the client version and exits.
- `-d, --debug`: This defaults to env `[HEATCLIENT_DEBUG]`.
- `-v, --verbose`: This prints more verbose output.
- `--api-timeout API_TIMEOUT`: This is the number of seconds to wait for an API response, which is set to system socket timeout by default.
- `--os-no-client-auth`: Do not contact keystone for a token; this argument defaults to env `[OS_NO_CLIENT_AUTH]`.
- `--heat-url HEAT_URL`: This defaults to env `[HEAT_URL]`.
- `--heat-api-version HEAT_API_VERSION`: This defaults to env `[HEAT_API_VERSION]` or 1.
- `--include-password`: This sends `os-username` and `os-password` to Heat.
- `-k, --insecure`: This explicitly allows the Heat client to perform "insecure SSL" (HTTPS) requests. The server's certificate will not be verified against any certificate authorities. This option should be used with caution.

- `--os-cert OS_CERT`: This is the path of certificate file to use in SSL connection. This file can optionally be prepended with the private key.

- `--cert-file OS_CERT`: This option is deprecated in the latest versions, therefore use `--os-cert` option instead of it.

- `--os-key OS_KEY`: The path of client key to use in SSL connection. This option is not necessary if your key is prepended to your `cert` file.

- `--key-file OS_KEY`: This option is being deprecated in the latest versions, therefore use `--os-key` option instead of it.

- `--os-cacert<ca-certificate-file>`: This is the path of CA TLS certificate(s) used to verify the remote server's certificate. Without this option, glance looks for the default system CA certificates.

- `--ca-file OS_CACERT`: This option is being deprecated in the latest versions, therefore use `--os-cacert` option instead of it.

- `--os-username OS_USERNAME`: This defaults to `env[OS_USERNAME]`.

- `--os-user-id OS_USER_ID`: This defaults to `env[OS_USER_ID]`.

- `--os-user-domain-id OS_USER_DOMAIN_ID`: This defaults to `env[OS_USER_DOMAIN_ID]`.

- `--os-user-domain-name OS_USER_DOMAIN_NAME`: This defaults to `env[OS_USER_DOMAIN_NAME]`.

- `--os-project-id OS_PROJECT_ID`: This is another way to specify the tenant ID. This option is mutually exclusive with `--os-tenant-id`. This defaults to `env[OS_PROJECT_ID]`.

- `--os-project-name OS_PROJECT_NAME`: This is another way to specify tenant name. This option is mutually exclusive with `--os-tenant-name`. This defaults to `env[OS_PROJECT_NAME]`.

- `--os-project-domain-id OS_PROJECT_DOMAIN_ID`: This defaults to `env[OS_PROJECT_DOMAIN_ID]`.

- `--os-project-domain-name OS_PROJECT_DOMAIN_NAME`: This defaults to `env[OS_PROJECT_DOMAIN_NAME]`.

- `--os-password OS_PASSWORD`: This defaults to `env[OS_PASSWORD]`.

- `--os-tenant-id OS_TENANT_ID`: This defaults to `env[OS_TENANT_ID]`.

- `--os-tenant-name OS_TENANT_NAME`: This defaults to `env[OS_TENANT_NAME]`.

- `--os-auth-url OS_AUTH_URL`: This defaults to `env[OS_AUTH_URL]`.

- `--os-region-name OS_REGION_NAME`: This defaults to `env[OS_REGION_NAME]`.

- `--os-auth-token OS_AUTH_TOKEN`: This defaults to env`[OS_AUTH_TOKEN]`.
- `--os-service-type OS_SERVICE_TYPE`: This defaults to env`[OS_SERVICE_TYPE]`.
- `--os-endpoint-type OS_ENDPOINT_TYPE`: This defaults to env`[OS_ENDPOINT_TYPE]`.

The subcommands of Heat can be implemented as follows:

- `heat action-check`: This checks whether the stack resources are in expected states. This is used as follows:

  heat action-check <NAME or ID>

  The positional arguments are `<NAME or ID>`, which denotes the name or the ID of the stack to be check.

- `heat action-resume`: This resumes the stack. It is used as:

  heat action-resume <NAME or ID>

  The positional arguments are `<NAME or ID>`, which denotes the name or ID of stack to resume.

- `heat action-suspend`: This suspends the stack. It is used as:

  heat action-suspend <NAME or ID>

  The positional arguments are `<NAME or ID>`, which represents the name or the ID of the stack to suspend.

- `heat build-info`: This retrieves the build information. It is used as:

  heat build-info

- `heat config-create`: This creates a software configuration. It is used as:

  heat config-create [-f <FILE or URL>] [-c <FILE or URL>]

  **   [-g <GROUP_NAME>]**

  <CONFIG_NAME>

  The positional argument is `<CONFIG_NAME>`, denoting the name of the configuration to create.

  The optional arguments are:

  - `-f <FILE or URL>, --definition-file <FILE or URL>`: This is the path to JSON/YAML containing map defining `<inputs>`, `<outputs>`, and `<options>`.

- ° `-c <FILE or URL>, --config-file <FILE or URL>`: This is the path to configuration script/data.

- ° `-g <GROUP_NAME>, --group <GROUP_NAME>`: This is the group name of the configuration tool expected by the config.

- `heat config-delete`: This deletes software configurations. It is used as:

`heat config-delete <ID> [<ID> ...]`

The positional argument is `<ID>`, which denotes the ID of the configurations to delete.

- `heat config-show`: This views details of a software configuration. It is used as:

`heat config-show [-c] <ID>`

The positional argument is `<ID>`, denoting the ID of the config.

The optional arguments are `-c` and `--config-only`, which only display the value of the `<config>` property.

- `heat deployment-create`:

```
heat deployment-create [-i<KEY=VALUE>] [-a <ACTION>] [-c <CONFIG>]
                       [-s <SERVER>] [-t <TRANSPORT>]
                       [--container <CONTAINER_NAME>]
                       [--timeout <TIMEOUT>]
<DEPLOY_NAME>
```

The positional argument is `<DEPLOY_NAME>`, denoting the name of the derived config associated with this deployment. This is used to apply a sort order to the list of configurations currently deployed to the server.

The optional arguments are as follows:

- ° `-i<KEY=VALUE>, --input-value <KEY=VALUE>`: This is the input value to set on the deployment. This can be specified multiple times.

- ° `-a <ACTION>, --action <ACTION>`: This is the name of action for this deployment. This can be a custom action, or one of these: CREATE, UPDATE, DELETE, SUSPEND, or RESUME.

- ° `-c <CONFIG>, --config<CONFIG>`: This is the ID of the configuration to deploy.

- ° `-s <SERVER>, --server <SERVER>`: This is the ID of the server being deployed to.

- -t <TRANSPORT>, --signal-transport <TRANSPORT>: This shows how the server should signal to Heat with the deployment output values. TEMP_URL_SIGNAL will create a Swift TempURL to be signaled via HTTP PUT. NO_SIGNAL will result in the resource going to the COMPLETE state without waiting for any signal.

- --container <CONTAINER_NAME>: This is the optional name of container to store TEMP_URL_SIGNAL objects in. If not specified, a container will be created with a name derived from the DEPLOY_NAME.

- --timeout <TIMEOUT>: This is the deployment timeout in minutes.

- heat deployment-delete: This deletes software deployments. It is used as:

```
heat deployment-delete <ID> [<ID> ...]
```

The positional argument is <ID>, representing the IDs of the deployments to delete.

- heat deployment-metadata-show: This gets deployment configuration metadata for the specified server. It is used as:

```
heat deployment-metadata-show <ID>
```

The positional argument is <ID>, representing the ID of the server to fetch deployments for.

- heat deployment-output-show: This shows a specific stack output. It is used as:

```
heat deployment-output-show [-a] [-F <FORMAT>] <ID> [<OUTPUT
NAME>]
```

The positional arguments are:

- <ID>: This is the ID deployment for which the output is displayed

- <OUTPUT NAME>: This is the name of an output to display

The optional arguments are:

- -a, --all: This displays all deployment outputs

- -F <FORMAT>, --format <FORMAT>: This is the output value format, for example: RAW, JSON

- heat deployment-show: This shows the details of a software deployment. It is used as:

```
heat deployment-show <ID>
```

The positional argument is <ID>, representing the ID of the deployment.

- `heat event-list`: This lists events for a stack. It is used as:

  ```
  heat event-list [-r <RESOURCE>] [-f <KEY1=VALUE1;KEY2=VALUE2...>]
                          [-l <LIMIT>] [-m <ID>]
  <NAME or ID>
  ```

  The positional arguments are `<NAME or ID>`, denoting the name or ID of stack to show the events for.

  The optional arguments are as follows:

  - `-r <RESOURCE>, --resource <RESOURCE>`: This is the name of the resource to filter events by.

  - `-f <KEY1=VALUE1;KEY2=VALUE2...>, --filters <KEY1=VALUE1;KEY2=VALUE2...>`: These are the filter parameters to apply on returned events. This can be specified multiple times, or once with parameters separated by a semicolon.

  - `-l <LIMIT>, --limit <LIMIT>`: This limits the number of events returned.

  - `-m <ID>, --marker <ID>`: This only returns events that appear after the given event ID.

- `heat event-show`: This describes the event. It is used as:

  ```
  heat event-show <NAME or ID><RESOURCE><EVENT>
  ```

  The positional arguments are as follows:

  - `<NAME or ID>`: This is the name or ID of stack to show the events for

  - `<RESOURCE>`: This is the name of the resource the event belongs to

  - `<EVENT>`: This is the ID of event to display details for

- `heat hook-clear`: This clears hooks on a given stack. It is used as:

  ```
  heat hook-clear [--pre-create] [--pre-update]
  <NAME or ID><RESOURCE> [<RESOURCE> ...]
  ```

  The positional arguments are as follows:

  - `<NAME or ID>`: This is the name or ID of the stack these resources belong to.

  - `<RESOURCE>`: These are the resource names with hooks to clear. Resources in nested stacks can be set using slash as a separator: `nested_stack/another/my_resource`. You can use wildcards to match multiple stacks or resources: `nested_stack/an*/*_resource`.

The optional arguments are as follows:

- ° `--pre-create`: This clears the pre-create hooks
- ° `--pre-update`: This clears the pre-update hooks

- `heat output-list`: This shows available outputs. It is used as:

```
heat output-list <NAME or ID>
```

The positional arguments are `<NAME or ID>`, denoting the name or ID of stack to query.

- `heat output-show`: This shows a specific stack output. It is used as:

```
heat output-show [-a] [-F <FORMAT>] <NAME or ID> [<OUTPUT NAME>]
```

The positional arguments are as follows:

- ° `<NAME or ID>`: This is the name or ID of stack to query
- ° `<OUTPUT NAME>`: This is the name of an output to display

The optional arguments are as follows:

- ° `-a, --all`: This displays all stack outputs
- ° `-F <FORMAT>, --format <FORMAT>`: The output value format, for example: JSON, RAW

- `heat resource-list`: This shows a list of resources belonging to a stack. It is used as:

```
heat resource-list [-n <DEPTH>] <NAME or ID>
```

The positional argument is `<NAME or ID>`, denoting the name or the ID of the stack to show the resources for.

Optional arguments are `-n <DEPTH>` and `--nested-depth <DEPTH>`, denoting the depth of nested stacks from which to display resources.

- `heat resource-metadata`: This lists the resource metadata. It is used as:

```
heat resource-metadata <NAME or ID><RESOURCE>
```

The positional arguments are:

- ° `<NAME or ID>`: This is the name or ID of stack to show the resource metadata for
- ° `<RESOURCE>`: This is the name of the resource to show the metadata for

- `heat resource-show`: This describes the resource. It is used as:

  `heat resource-show <NAME or ID><RESOURCE>`

  The positional arguments are as follows:

  - `<NAME or ID>`: This is the name or the ID of the stack to show the resource for
  - `<RESOURCE>`: This is the name of the resource to show the details for

- `heat resource-signal`: This sends a signal to the resource. It is used as:

  `heat resource-signal [-D <DATA>] [-f <FILE>] <NAME or ID><RESOURCE>`

  The positional arguments are as follows:

  - `<NAME or ID>`: This is the name or the ID of the stack the resource belongs to
  - `<RESOURCE>`: This is the name of the resource to signal

  The optional arguments are as follows:

  - `-D <DATA>, --data <DATA>`: This is the JSON data to send to the signal handler
  - `-f <FILE>, --data-file <FILE>`: This is the file containing JSON data to send to the signal handler

- `heat resource-type-list`: This is the list the available resource types. It is used as:

  `heat resource-type-list`

- `heat resource-type-show`: This shows the resource type. It is used as:

  `heat resource-type-show <RESOURCE_TYPE>`

  The positional argument is `<RESOURCE_TYPE>`, denoting the resource type to get the details for.

- `heat resource-type-template`: This generates a template based on a resource type. It is used as:

  `heat resource-type-template [-F <FORMAT>] <RESOURCE_TYPE>`

  The positional argument is`<RESOURCE_TYPE>`, denoting the resource type to generate a template for.

The optional arguments are `-F <FORMAT>` and `--format <FORMAT>`, denoting the template output format. This is the output format. It can be either JSON or YAML.

- `heat service-list`: This lists the Heat engines. It is used as:

`heat service-list`

- `heat snapshot-delete`: This deletes a snapshot of a stack. It is used as:

`heat snapshot-delete <NAME or ID><SNAPSHOT>`

The positional arguments are:

- `<NAME or ID>`: This is the name or the ID of the stack containing the snapshot.

- `<SNAPSHOT>`: This command takes the numeric ID of the snapshot that we want to delete. We need to provide the ID of the snapshot that we want to delete.

- `heat snapshot-list`: This lists the snapshots of a stack. It is used as:

`heat snapshot-list <NAME or ID>`

The positional argument is `<NAME or ID>`, denoting the name or ID of the stack containing the snapshots.

- `heat snapshot-show`: This shows a snapshot of the stack. It is used as:

`heat snapshot-show <NAME or ID><SNAPSHOT>`

The positional arguments are as follows:

- `<NAME or ID>`: This is the name or the ID of the stack containing the snapshot

- `<SNAPSHOT>`: This is the ID of the snapshot to show

- `heat stack-abandon`: This abandons the stack. This will delete the record of the stack from Heat, but will not delete any of the underlying resources. This prints an adoptable JSON representation of the stack to stdout or a file on success. It is used as:

`heat stack-abandon [-O <FILE>] <NAME or ID>`

The positional argument is `<NAME or ID>`, denoting the name or ID of stack to abandon.

The optional arguments are `-O <FILE>` and `--output-file <FILE>`, denoting the file to output the abandon result. If the option is specified, the result will be output into `<FILE>`.

- `heat stack-adopt`: This adopts a stack. It is used as:

```
heat stack-adopt [-e <FILE or URL>] [-c <TIMEOUT>] [-t <TIMEOUT>]
                        [-a <FILE or URL>] [-r]
                        [-P <KEY1=VALUE1;KEY2=VALUE2...>]
<STACK_NAME>
```

The positional argument is `<STACK_NAME>`, denoting the name of the stack to adopt.

The optional arguments are as follows:

  ○ `e <FILE or URL>, --environment-file <FILE or URL>`: This is the path to the environment, which can be specified multiple times

  ○ `-c <TIMEOUT>, --create-timeout <TIMEOUT>`: Stack creation timeout in minutes; `DEPRECATED` use `--timeout` instead

  ○ `-t <TIMEOUT>, --timeout <TIMEOUT>`: Stack creation timeout in minutes

  ○ `-a <FILE or URL>, --adopt-file <FILE or URL>`: This is the path to adopt stack data file

  ○ `-r, --enable-rollback`: This enables rollback on create/update failure

  ○ `-P <KEY1=VALUE1;KEY2=VALUE2...>, --parameters <KEY1=VALUE1;KEY2=VALUE2...>`: These are the parameter values used to create the stack; they can be specified multiple times, or once with parameters separated by a semicolon

- `heat stack-cancel-update`: This cancels updates of the stack that are currently running. It is used as:

```
heat stack-cancel-update <NAME or ID>
```

The positional argument is `<NAME or ID>`, denoting the name or ID of stack to cancel update for.

- `heat stack-create`: This creates the stack. It is used as:

```
heat stack-create [-f <FILE>] [-e <FILE or URL>]
                        [--pre-create <RESOURCE>] [-u <URL>] [-o
<URL>]
                        [-c <TIMEOUT>] [-t <TIMEOUT>] [-r]
                        [-P <KEY1=VALUE1;KEY2=VALUE2...>] [-Pf
<KEY=VALUE>]
<STACK_NAME>
```

The positional argument is `<STACK_NAME>`, which denotes the name of the stack to be created.

The optional arguments are as follows:

- ○ `-f <FILE>, --template-file <FILE>`: This is the path to the template.

- ○ `-e <FILE or URL>, --environment-file <FILE or URL>`: This is the path to the environment; it can be specified multiple times.

- ○ `--pre-create <RESOURCE>`: This is the name of a resource to set a pre-create hook to. Resources in nested stacks can be set using slash as a separator: `nested_stack/another/my_resource`. You can use wildcards to match multiple stacks or resources: `nested_stack/an*/*_resource`. This can be specified multiple times.

- ○ `-u <URL>, --template-url<URL>`: This is the URL of the template.

- ○ `-o <URL>, --template-object <URL>`: This is the URL used to retrieve template object (for example, from Swift).

- ○ `-c <TIMEOUT>, --create-timeout <TIMEOUT>`: Stack creation timeout in minutes. DEPRECATED use `--timeout` instead.

- ○ `-t <TIMEOUT>, --timeout <TIMEOUT>`: Stack creation timeout in minutes.

- ○ `-r, --enable-rollback`: This enables rollback on create/update failure.

- ○ `-P <KEY1=VALUE1;KEY2=VALUE2...>, --parameters <KEY1=VALUE1;KEY2=VALUE2...>`: These are parameter values used to create the stack. This can be specified multiple times, or once with parameters separated by a semicolon.

- ○ `-Pf <KEY=VALUE>, --parameter-file <KEY=VALUE>`: These are parameter values from the file used to create the stack. This can be specified multiple times. The parameter value will be the content of the file.

- `heat stack-delete`: This deletes the stack(s). It is used as:

  ```
  heat stack-delete <NAME or ID> [<NAME or ID> ...]
  ```

  This command takes either the name of the stack or the numeric ID of the stack that we want to delete.

- `heat stack-list`: This lists the user's stacks. It is used as:

  ```
  heat stack-list [-s] [-n] [-f <KEY1=VALUE1;KEY2=VALUE2...>]
                  [-1 <LIMIT>] [-m <ID>] [-g] [-o]
  ```

The optional arguments are as follows:

- ○ `-s`, `--show-deleted`: This includes soft-deleted stacks in the stack listing.

- ○ `-n`, `--show-nested`: This includes nested stacks in the stack listing.

- ○ `-f <KEY1=VALUE1;KEY2=VALUE2...>`, `--filters <KEY1=VALUE1;KEY2=VALUE2...>`: This filters parameters to apply on returned stacks. This can be specified multiple times, or once with parameters separated by a semicolon.

- ○ `-l <LIMIT>`, `--limit <LIMIT>`: This limits the number of stacks returned.

- ○ `-m <ID>`, `--marker <ID>`: This only returns stacks that appear after the given stack ID.

- ○ `-g`, `--global-tenant`: This displays stacks from all tenants. Operation only authorized for users who's policy match the policy in Heat's `policy.json` file.

- ○ `-o`, `--show-owner`: This displays information about the stack owner. This is automatically enabled when using `--global-tenant`.

- `heat stack-preview`: This previews the stack. It is used as:

```
heat stack-preview [-f <FILE>] [-e <FILE or URL>] [-u <URL>] [-o
<URL>]

                        [-t <TIMEOUT>] [-r]

                        [-P <KEY1=VALUE1;KEY2=VALUE2...>] [-Pf
<KEY=VALUE>]

<STACK_NAME>
```

The positional argument is `<STACK_NAME>` which denotes the name of the stack to preview.

The optional arguments are as follows:

- ○ `-f <FILE>`, `--template-file <FILE>`: This is the path to the template.

- ○ `-e <FILE or URL>`, `--environment-file <FILE or URL>`: This is the path to the environment; it can be specified multiple times.

- ○ `-u <URL>`, `--template-url<URL>`: This is the URL of the template.

- ○ `-o <URL>`, `--template-object <URL>`: This is the URL to retrieve the template object (for example, from Swift).

- `-t <TIMEOUT>, --timeout <TIMEOUT>`: Stack creation timeout in minutes. This is only used during validation in preview.

- `-r, --enable-rollback`: This enables rollback on failure. This option is not used during preview and exists only for symmetry with stack- create.

- `-P <KEY1=VALUE1;KEY2=VALUE2...>, --parameters <KEY1=VALUE1;KEY2=VALUE2...>`: These are the parameter values used to preview the stack. This can be specified multiple times, or once with parameters separated by semicolon.

- `-Pf <KEY=VALUE>, --parameter-file <KEY=VALUE>`: These are parameter values from the file used to create the stack. This can be specified multiple times. Parameter value would be the content of the file.

- `heat stack-restore`: This restores the snapshot of a stack. It is used as:

  `heat stack-restore <NAME or ID><SNAPSHOT>`

  The positional arguments are as follows:

  - `<NAME or ID>`: This is the name or ID of the stack containing the snapshot

  - `<SNAPSHOT>`: We need to provide the ID of the snapshot that we want to restore

- `heat stack-show`: Describe the stack. It is used as:

  `heat stack-show <NAME or ID>`

  The positional argument is `<NAME or ID>`, for which we will provide either the name or the numeric ID of the stack that we want to describe.

- `heat stack-snapshot`: This makes a snapshot of a stack. It is used as:

  `heat stack-snapshot [-n <NAME>] <NAME or ID>`

  The positional argument is `<NAME or ID>`, denoting the name or the ID of the stack to snapshot.

  The optional arguments are `-n <NAME>` and `--name <NAME>`, which denotes the name given to the snapshot.

- heat stack-update: This updates the stack. It is used as:

```
heat stack-update [-f <FILE>] [-e <FILE or URL>]
                         [--pre-update <RESOURCE>] [-u <URL>] [-o
<URL>]
                         [-t <TIMEOUT>] [-r] [--rollback <VALUE>]
                         [-P <KEY1=VALUE1;KEY2=VALUE2...>] [-Pf
<KEY=VALUE>]
                         [-x] [-c <PARAMETER>]
<NAME or ID>
```

The positional argument is `<NAME or ID>`, denoting the name or ID of stack to be updated.

The optional arguments are as follows:

- `-f <FILE>`, `--template-file <FILE>`: This is the path to the template.

- `-e <FILE or URL>`, `--environment-file <FILE or URL>`: This is the path to the environment, which can be specified multiple times.

- `--pre-update <RESOURCE>`: This is the name of a resource to set a pre-update hook to. Resources in nested stacks can be set using slash as a separator: `nested_stack/another/my_resource`. You can use wildcards to match multiple stacks or resources: `nested_stack/an*/*_resource`. This can be specified multiple times.

- `-u <URL>`, `--template-url<URL>`: This is the URL of the template.

- `-o <URL>`, `--template-object <URL>`: This is the URL to retrieve the template object (for example, from Swift).

- `-t <TIMEOUT>`, `--timeout <TIMEOUT>`: Stack update timeout in minutes.

- `-r`, `--enable-rollback`: This is deprecated. Use `--rollback` argument instead. This enables rollback on the stack update failure. Note that the default behavior is now to use the rollback value of existing stack.

- `--rollback <VALUE>`: This sets rollback on update failure. Values (`'1'`, `'t'`, `'true'`, `'on'`, `'y'`, `'yes'`) set rollback to `enable`. Values (`'0'`, `'f'`, `'false'`, `'off'`, `'n'`, `'no'`) set rollback to `disabled`. Default is to use the value of existing stack to be updated.

- ○ `-P <KEY1=VALUE1;KEY2=VALUE2...>, --parameters <KEY1=VALUE1;KEY2=VALUE2...>`: These are parameter values used to create the stack. This can be specified multiple times, or once with parameters separated by a semicolon.

  - ○ `-Pf <KEY=VALUE>, --parameter-file <KEY=VALUE>`: These are the parameter values from file used to create the stack. This can be specified multiple times. The parameter value will be the content of the file.

  - ○ `-x, --existing`: Reuse the set of parameters of the current stack. Parameters specified in `--parameters` will patch over the existing values in the current stack. Parameters omitted will keep the existing values.

  - ○ `-c <PARAMETER>, --clear-parameter <PARAMETER>`: Remove the parameters from the set of parameters of current stack for the stack-update. The default value in the template will be used. This can be specified multiple times.

- `heat template-show`: Get the template for the specified stack. It is used as:

  `heat template-show <NAME or ID>`

  The positional argument is `<NAME or ID>`, denoting the name or ID of stack to get the template for.

- `heat template-validate`: This validates a template with parameters. It is used as:

  `heat template-validate [-u <URL>] [-f <FILE>] [-e <FILE or URL>]`
  `[-o <URL>]`

  The optional arguments are as follows:

  - ○ `-u <URL>, --template-url<URL>`: This is the URL of the template

  - ○ `-f <FILE>, --template-file <FILE>`: This is the path to the template

  - ○ `-e <FILE or URL>, --environment-file <FILE or URL>`: This is the path to the environment, which can be specified multiple times

  - ○ `-o <URL>, --template-object <URL>`: This is the URL used to retrieve template object (for example, from Swift)

The Heat basic workflow

Two kinds of workflows are supported by Heat. Using the first type of workflow, Heat starts several tasks in parallel and waits till they are completed. In the second workflow type, a parallelized task is run for an arbitrary dependency graph.

The following diagram shows a basic workflow for the OpenStack Heat component:

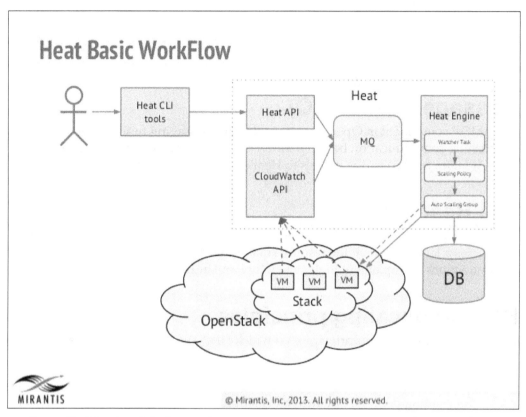

Source: The Mirantis website (`http://openstack.prov12n.com/openstack-heat-concepts-architecture-and-workflow/`)

The Heat CLI tools

The Heat CLI tools (already described in the previous sections) are used to send the queries to the Heat engine. This is done via the Heat API and the CloudWatch API.

The Heat API

The Heat API implements the REST API for OpenStack. It is used to send queries to the Heat engine via the AMPQ messaging system. This can be initiated from using Heat CLI Tools or a web application such as the horizon dashboard.

The Heat CloudWatch API

The Heat CloudWatch API component is used to get the metrics from the stacks. It actually refers to the AWS CloudWatch service. The Ceilometer component of OpenStack actually replaces it.

Message queue (MQ)

The AMQP component in OpenStack provides the messaging functionality for establishing communication between different components in OpenStack. The Heat API uses MQ to send messages to Heat engine for orchestration activities.

The Heat engine

The Heat engine provides the actual orchestration functionality and is the core part. It provides a layer on which the resource integration is implemented. It also contains the abstractions to implement high availability and autoscaling.

Heat autoscaling principles

The following are the main principles on which Heat autoscaling features are based upon:

- Heat agents are installed on individual VMs. These agents are responsible for sending periodic updates to the monitoring component (Ceilometer) after specific intervals.

- The monitoring component (CloudWatch or Ceilometer) takes the responsibility of communicating between the VMs and the Heat engine.

- The Heat engine (the core part) provides the Orchestration and autoscaling features.

JeOS

JeOS (Just Enough Operating System) is a term used to define a highly customized version of an operating system designed for a specific application. It is pronounced "juice."

It is normally referred to a VM built for a specific application. This helps to use VMs with small images while fulfilling the requirements of the given application.

A Heat JeOS can be created while using the diskimage-builder software available at `https://github.com/openstack/diskimage-builder`.

Summary

In this chapter, we discussed the detailed functionality provided by the Orchestration component for OpenStack Heat. We explained the basic architecture that builds the Heat orchestration service. We also explained the command-line parameters and optional arguments required by the Heat CLI component. In the later sections of this module, we discussed the message flow for Heat and the role played by each component in the flow.

In the next chapter, we will create and delete a stack and see the various methods to manage stacks.

6
Managing Heat

In the previous chapter, we covered Heat functionality in detail. We also discussed the basic architecture of Heat and the main components that build up the Orchestration service for OpenStack. Then, we covered the command-line arguments accepted by Heat CLI. Finally, we explained the message flow for Heat.

In this chapter, we will cover the following objectives:

- Heat and DevStack
- Get the stack list
- The event stack list
- Create a stack
- Delete a stack
- The template structure
- The CloudFormation template

Heat and DevStack

DevStack provides a set of scripts for automated installation of OpenStack on Ubuntu as well as Fedora Linux. It is a tool to help OpenStack developers to quickly set up an OpenStack environment using scripts. These scripts automatically download or clone the required packages and repositories from the OpenStack website that are necessary for setting up an OpenStack cloud.

One drawback with this approach is that the environment is not persistent across server reboots. There are scripts such as `rejoin-stack` that need to be run to recreate the environment after a server has been rebooted.

Therefore, DevStack is not recommended for a production install. However, it can only be used for testing and development purpose, where an OpenStack environment is created and destroyed several times. When OpenStack is required in a purely development environment, other methods of installation can be used.

DevStack can also be configured for enabling and using Heat services. This can be done using the `local.conf` file under the DevStack directory. The following is the complete step-by-step procedure to install OpenStack including Heat while using the DevStack scripts on Ubuntu 14.04 LTS:

1. Prepare a machine (or a VM) running Ubuntu 14.04 LTS and install `openssh-server`:

   root@ubuntu$ apt-get install openssh-server

   We'll get the following output for this command:

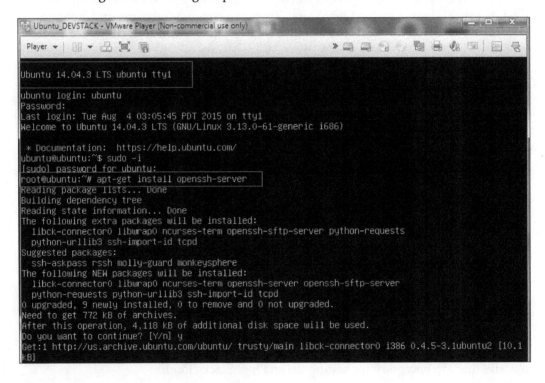

2. Next, the `git` client needs to be installed for cloning the `devstack` repository to the local machine with the following command:

```
root@ubuntu$ sudo apt-get install git
```

For this command, we will get the following output:

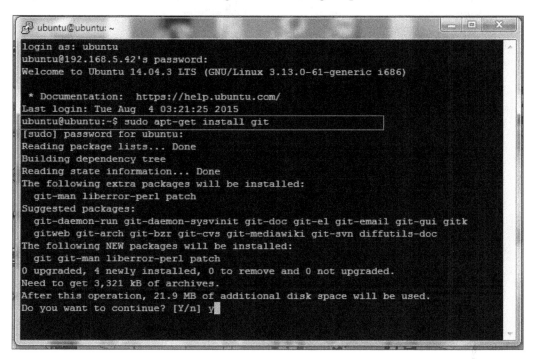

```
login as: ubuntu
ubuntu@192.168.5.42's password:
Welcome to Ubuntu 14.04.3 LTS (GNU/Linux 3.13.0-61-generic i686)

 * Documentation:  https://help.ubuntu.com/
Last login: Tue Aug  4 03:21:25 2015
ubuntu@ubuntu:~$ sudo apt-get install git
[sudo] password for ubuntu:
Reading package lists... Done
Building dependency tree
Reading state information... Done
The following extra packages will be installed:
  git-man liberror-perl patch
Suggested packages:
  git-daemon-run git-daemon-sysvinit git-doc git-el git-email git-gui gitk
  gitweb git-arch git-bzr git-cvs git-mediawiki git-svn diffutils-doc
The following NEW packages will be installed:
  git git-man liberror-perl patch
0 upgraded, 4 newly installed, 0 to remove and 0 not upgraded.
Need to get 3,321 kB of archives.
After this operation, 21.9 MB of additional disk space will be used.
Do you want to continue? [Y/n] y
```

3. After installing Git, the `devstack` repository from OpenStack website needs to be cloned using the following command:

```
ubuntu@ubntu$ git clone https://git.openstack.org/openstack-dev/
devstack
```

The output for this is shown in the following screenshot:

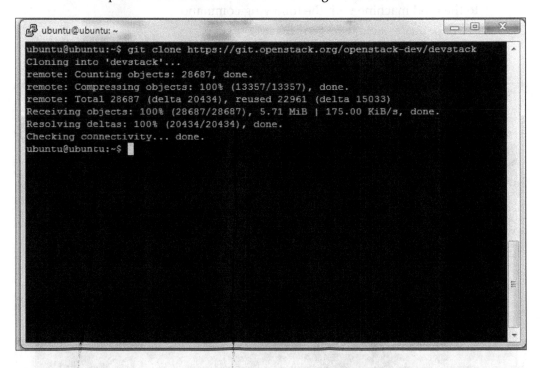

4. Once the `devstack` folder is cloned to the local machine, we need to use a copy of the `local.conf` file, which is available under samples folder inside the `devstack` folder. To make a copy, we use the `cp` command as follows:

   ```
   ubuntu@ubntu$ cd devstack/samples/
   ```

   ```
   ubuntu@ubntu$  cp local.conf ../
   ```

   The output will be as shown in the following screenshot:

   ```
   ubuntu@ubuntu:~$ cd devstack/samples/
   ubuntu@ubuntu:~/devstack/samples$ ls
   local.conf  local.sh
   ubuntu@ubuntu:~/devstack/samples$ cp local.conf  ../
   ubuntu@ubuntu:~/devstack/samples$
   ```

5. Next, we need to configure the correct parameters for different passwords to be used with OpenStack. For this purpose, we will open the new copy of `local.conf` using the `vi` command as follows:

ubuntu@ubntu$ cd ../

ubuntu@ubntu$ vi local.conf

The output will be as shown in the following screenshot:

6. The passwords can be set under the `[local|localrc]` section as follows:

```
[[local|localrc]]
SERVICE_TOKEN=cloud123
ADMIN_PASSWORD=cloud123
MYSQL_PASSWORD=cloud123
RABBIT_PASSWORD=cloud123
SERVICE_PASSWORD=$ADMIN_PASSWORD
```

The following screenshot shows an example of this process:

```
# The ``localrc`` section replaces the old ``localrc`` configuration file.
# Note that if ``localrc`` is present it will be used in favor of this section.
[[local|localrc]]

# Minimal Contents
# ----------------

# While ``stack.sh`` is happy to run without ``localrc``, devlife is better when
# there are a few minimal variables set:

# If the ``SERVICE_TOKEN`` and ``*_PASSWORD`` variables are not set
# here you will be prompted to enter values for them by ``stack.sh``
# and they will be added to ``local.conf``.
SERVICE_TOKEN=cloud123
ADMIN_PASSWORD=cloud123
MYSQL_PASSWORD=cloud123
RABBIT_PASSWORD=cloud123
SERVICE_PASSWORD=$ADMIN_PASSWORD
```

7. After setting the passwords, we need to enable automated installation of Heat and its services along with the OpenStack components. To achieve this, we need to configure the following parameters:

```
[[local|localrc]]
SERVICE_TOKEN=cloud123
ADMIN_PASSWORD=cloud123
MYSQL_PASSWORD=cloud123
RABBIT_PASSWORD=cloud123
SERVICE_PASSWORD=$ADMIN_PASSWORD
HOST_IP=192.168.5.42
#ENABLE  HEAT services
enable_service h-eng h-api h-api-cfn h-api-cw
# ENABLE CEILOMETER
CEILOMETER_BACKEND=mongodb
enable_service ceilometer-acompute ceilometer-acentral ceilometer-collector ceilometer-api
enable_service ceilometer-alarm-notifier ceilometer-alarm-evaluator
```

Additionally, the Ceilometer service can be enabled in the same section. The correct parameters for enabling Ceilometer are also displayed in the following screenshot:

8. Next, the changes need be saved and exited and the script called stack.sh can be called, as shown in the following screenshot:

9. If everything goes as it should, then the script should complete the installation of OpenStack, including Heat (Orchestration). The OpenStack dashboard (Horizon) can be seen using the URL at http://IP_ADDRESS_OF_YOUR_HOST.

Here, IP_ADDRESS_OF_YOUR_HOST needs to be replaced with the correct IP address of the machine on which DevStack is installed.

The event stack list

As explained earlier, events are associated with a stack. As explained in *Chapter 3, Stack Group of Connected Cloud Resources*, Heat uses the term "stack" to define a collection of resources combined together into a group for orchestration or scaling. These resources may include **virtual machine (VM)** instances, routers, switches, ports, router interfaces, security groups, subnets, storage volumes, and so on.

The command used to list events associated with a stack is as follows:

```
Ubuntu@ubunut $ heat event-list [-r <RESOURCE>] [-f
<KEY1=VALUE1;KEY2=VALUE2...>]
                        [-l <LIMIT>] [-m <ID>]
                        <NAME or ID>
```

Where:

Parameter	Description
<NAME or ID>	This represents the name or ID of the stack for which events needed to be listed.
-r <RESOURCE>, --resource <RESOURCE>	This represents the name of resource for filtering the events.
-f <KEY1=VALUE1;KEY2=VALUE2...>, --filters <KEY1=VALUE1;KEY2=VALUE2...>	This is used to apply filter parameters on the returned events. One or more *key=value* pairs can be specified by separating them with a semicolon.
-l <LIMIT>, --limit <LIMIT>	This is used to limit the number of events returned.
-m <ID>, --marker <ID>	This is used as a marker to return events after the given event ID.

The following screenshot shows this:

```
ubuntu@ubuntu~$ heat event-list Single-Server-Stack
+---------------------+----+-----------------------+-----------------+----------------------+
| logical_resource_id | id | resource_status_reason | resource_status | event_time          |
+---------------------+----+-----------------------+-----------------+----------------------+
| TestDatabase        | 1  | state changed         | IN_PROGRESS     | 2013-04-03T23:22:09Z |
| TestDatabase        | 2  | state changed         | CREATE_COMPLETE | 2013-04-03T23:25:56Z |
+---------------------+----+-----------------------+-----------------+----------------------+
```

Get the stack list

The Heat `stack-list` command is used to list all the stacks created under Heat domain. The following screenshot is an output of this command:

```
ubuntu@ubuntu:~$ heat stack-list
+--------------------------------------+--------------------+-----------------+----------------------+
| id                                   | stack_name         | stack_status    | creation_time        |
+--------------------------------------+--------------------+-----------------+----------------------+
| bd2c230-b02a-45d8-9f16-88c9a9f64d2d  | Single-Server-Stack | CREATE_COMPLETE | 2015-08-23T19:41:05Z |
+--------------------------------------+--------------------+-----------------+----------------------+
```

Create a stack

A new stack can be created using a template file or with help of cURL. We will use an example template file to create a stack. Let's suppose we have a template file named `single_server.template`. We will use the following command to create a stack:

ubuntu@ubuntu~$ heat stack-create Single-Server-Stack --template-file single_server.template

The output will be something similar to the one shown in the following screenshot:

```
ubuntu@ubuntu:~$ heat stack-create Single-Server-Stack --template-file single_server.template

+--------------------------------------+--------------------+------------------+----------------------+
| id                                   | stack_name         | stack_status     | creation_time        |
+--------------------------------------+--------------------+------------------+----------------------+
| 3bd2c230-b02a-45d8-9f16-88c9a9f64d2d | Single-Server-Stack | CREATE_IN_PROGRESS | 2015-08-24T20:12:47Z |
+--------------------------------------+--------------------+------------------+----------------------+
```

The `stack-create` command can also be used for validating a template file without creating an actual stack. This can be a dry run to test whether there are no errors in the template file. The following is the command used to achieve this:

```
ubuntu@ubuntu~$ heat stack-create Single-Server-Stack --template-file
single_server.template
```

Show stack details

Another useful command is to show the detailed contents of a stack. A stack is a collection of resources. The following command can be used to show the details about a stack:

```
ubuntu@ubuntu~$ heat resource-list Single-Server-Stack
```

The following screenshot displays the output:

```
ubuntu@ubuntu~$ heat resource-list Single-Server-Stack
+---------------------+-----------------+-----------------+----------------------+
| logical_resource_id | resource_type   | resource_status | updated_time         |
+---------------------+-----------------+-----------------+----------------------+
| TestDatabase        | AWS::EC2::Instance | CREATE_COMPLETE | 2013-04-03T23:25:56Z |
+---------------------+-----------------+-----------------+----------------------+
```

Show resource details

The resources in a stack can be listed using the following command:

```
ubuntu@ubuntu~$ heat resource-show Single-Server-Stack TestDatabase
```

Here, `TestDatabase` is the name of resource created under the stack `Single-Server-Stack`.

The following screenshot displays the output of the preceding command:

```
ubuntu@ubuntu~$ heat stack-show Single-Server-Stack
+---------------------+-----------------------------------------------------------------------------------------------------------+
| capabilities        | []                                                                                                        |
| creation_time       | 2014-01-24T20:12:47Z                                                                                      |
| description         | No description                                                                                            |
| disable_rollback    | True                                                                                                      |
| id                  | 3bd2c230-b02a-45d8-9f16-88c9a9f64d2d                                                                      |
| links               | http://ord.orchestration.api.rackspacecloud.com/v1/1234/stacks/Single-Server-Stack/3bd2c230-b02a-45d8-9f16-88c9a9f64d2d |
| notification_topics | []                                                                                                        |
| outputs             | [                                                                                                         |
|                     |   {                                                                                                       |
|                     |     "output_value": "23.253.88.131",                                                                      |
|                     |     "description": "public IP address of the deployed compute instance",                                  |
|                     |     "output_key": "public_ip"                                                                             |
|                     |   }                                                                                                       |
|                     | ]                                                                                                         |
| parameters          | {                                                                                                         |
|                     |   "OS::stack_name": "Single-Server-Stack",                                                                |
|                     |   "OS::stack_id": "3bd2c230-b02a-45d8-9f16-88c9a9f64d2d"                                                  |
|                     | }                                                                                                         |
| stack_name          | Single-Server-Stack                                                                                       |
| stack_status        | CREATE_COMPLETE                                                                                           |
| stack_status_reason | Stack CREATE completed successfully                                                                       |
| template_description| No description                                                                                            |
| timeout_mins        | 60                                                                                                        |
| updated_time        | None                                                                                                      |
+---------------------+-----------------------------------------------------------------------------------------------------------+
```

Update a stack

The following command can be executed to update the stack that we already created in previous sections:

```
ubuntu@ubuntu~$    heat stack-update Single-Server-Stack -
template-file=/path/to/templates/single_server.template
--parameters="InstanceType=m1.large;DBUsername=wp;DBPassword=verybadpassw
ord;KeyName=heat_key;LinuxDistribution=F17"
```

An example run is shown in the following screenshot:

```
ubuntu@ubuntu~$ heat stack-update Single-Server-Stack \
> --template-file=/path/to/templates/Single_wordpress_instace.template \
> --parameters="InstanceType=m1.large;DBUsername=wp;\
> DBPassword=verybadpassword;KeyName=heat_key;LinuxDistribution=F17"

+----------------------------------------+-----------------------+-----------------+----------------------+
| id                                     | stack_name            | stack_status    | creation_time        |
+----------------------------------------+-----------------------+-----------------+----------------------+
| 4c712026-dcd5-4664-90b8-0915494c1332   | Single-Server-Stack   | UPDATE_COMPLETE | 2013-04-03T23:22:08Z |
| 7edc7480-bda5-4e1c-9d5d-f567d3b6a050   | Multiple-Server-stack | CREATE_FAILED   | 2013-04-03T23:28:20Z |
+----------------------------------------+-----------------------+-----------------+----------------------+
```

Delete a stack

A stack can be deleted by using the command heat stack-delete. The following is the command syntax:

```
ubuntu@ubuntu~$ heat stack-delete Single-Server-Stack
```

The output for this command is shown in the following screenshot:

```
ubuntu@ubuntu:~$ heat stack-delete Single-Server-Stack
+-------------------------------------+----------------------+-------------------+----------------------+
| id                                  | stack_name           | stack_status      | creation_time        |
+-------------------------------------+----------------------+-------------------+----------------------+
| bd2c230-b02a-45d8-9f16-88c9a9f64d2d | Single-Server-Stack  | DELETE_IN_PROGRESS | 2015-08-23T19:41:05Z |
+-------------------------------------+----------------------+-------------------+----------------------+
```

The template structure

HOT (**Heat Orchestration Template**) is a native format that has been recently developed to be used with Heat. Besides HOT, Heat is also compatible with AWS CloudFormation templates. Heat Orchestration Templates uses the YAML format. The following is the structure of a basic HOT template:

```
heat_template_version: 2013-05-23
description:
# This describes the purpose of template
parameter_groups:
# Here input parameters groups are defined in an order
parameters:
#In this section, input parameters are declared in an order
resources:
# Template resources are declared in this section
outputs:
# In this section output parameters are declared.
```

The different parameters of a basic HOT template are:

- `heat_template_version`: This parameter is used to mention the version of the template. The date is the release date of OpenStack (for example, Juno, Icehouse, and so on).

- `description`: This parameter is used to explaining the purpose of this template.

- `parameter_groups`: This section explains the input parameter groups and their order. It is not a mandatory section.

- `parameters`: This section is also optional and is used to mention the actual parameter that would be provided while instantiating this template.

- **resources**: This section should contain at least one resource that this template will use when instantiated.
- **outputs**: The output parameters can be defined in this section. Here those output parameters would be mentioned, which would be available to the user upon instantiation of this template.

The CloudFormation template

The AWS CloudFormation template is has the JSON format and explains the infrastructure. The only mandatory section is the Resources section and all others are optional. The template as well as the subsections are enclosed in braces {}. The following is an example of the CloudFormation template:

```
{
  "AWSTemplateFormatVersion" : "version date",

  "Description" : "JSON string",

  "Metadata" : {
    template metadata
  },

  "Parameters" : {
    set of parameters
  },

  "Mappings" : {
    set of mappings
  },

  "Conditions" : {
    set of conditions
  },

  "Resources" : {
    set of resources
  },

  "Outputs" : {
    set of outputs
  }
}
```

The AWS template format version

The `AWSTemplateFormatVersion` section provides the version of OpenStack to which this template conforms to. This value is not mandatory. The version can be different from the API version.

Description

The `Description` parameter is also optional that specifies the definition of template and the purpose it will serve.

Metadata

The `Metadata` section contains additional information about the template. It is mentioned in the form of JSON objects.

Parameters

The `Parameters` section explains those parameters that are passed to the template during execution time or runtime. These are also optional.

Mappings

The `Mappings` section includes a mapping of key value pairs that are used to specify conditional parameter settings. It is known as hashes or dictionaries in some programming languages and also known as lookup tables in some cases. To find a match for a value against a key, the `Fn::FindInMap` intrinsic function is used under the `Resources` or `Outputs` section.

Conditions

The `Conditions` section defines conditions for controlling the creation of resources during the creation time of stacks or even during updating a stack. A condition can be set to create a resource such as an additional storage disk depending upon the nature of stack being created or updated.

Resources

The `Resources` section defines the resources, including storage service, compute instances, or floating IP addresses, and so on.

Outputs

The Outputs section is used to define output settings and values to be returned as outputs when a client requests.

Summary

This chapter covered installing DevStack with Heat support. The local.conf file needs to be configured to enable Heat services with DevStack. Heat supports native HOT format as well as AWS CloudFormation templates. Stacks can be created, deleted, and viewed using the Heat command line (Heat CLI). HOT uses a YAML formatted file to generate templates while AWS CloudFormation uses JSON format where the sections are enclosed in braces. Heat stacks can be created and destroyed using the Heat CLI.

7
Troubleshooting Heat

In the previous chapters, we talked about how to set up and run OpenStack Heat in detail. We tried to cover almost every aspect of Heat. This included the basic architecture of Heat, the main components of Heat, which build up the Orchestration service for OpenStack, Heat message flow, and the command-line arguments accepted by the Heat CLI. The Heat template formats and structures supported by Heat were also discussed. Finally, we explained the message flow for Heat.

In this chapter, we will focus on troubleshooting the issues encountered with Heat. The issues discussed in this chapter are:

- VM instances cannot connect to the external network or the Internet
- Error received during installation: Unable to write random state
- Timeout error received while running `jeos_create` during customization
- A template running with incorrect parameters cannot be deleted
- Error: Internal error process exited while connecting to the monitor
- It takes too long to create a JeOS
- Error: Quota exceeded: code=InstanceLimitExceeded (HTTP 413)
- Error: Response from Keystone does not contain a Heat endpoint
- Error: Internal Server Error
- Error: Provided KeyName not registered with nova
- A template is not working after editing
- Instances shutdown immediately after creation
- Yum update fails with dependency problems related to the `oz` package
- Failed to start qpidd
- OpenStack daemons can't connect to qpidd

- Ubuntu VMs cannot receive DHCP assignments from hosts running CentOS/Fedora
- Debugging OpenStack Heat
- Heat list returns 503 error
- Heat list hangs up
- Troubleshooting common OpenStack errors

VM instances cannot connect to the external network or the Internet

If the virtual machine instances in OpenStack that were created using Heat are not able to communicate with the outside world, then there is a chance that the following configuration is missing in the Nova configuration file:

```
flat_interface = eth0
public_interface = eth0
```

These parameters should be set properly according to the physical interfaces on the host machine. In this example, it is assumed that eth0 is the public facing interface on a physical host where all-in-one OpenStack is installed.

It is necessary to adjust the name of the physical interface according to the actual configuration on the physical host machine.

If these configuration parameters are not set properly, then Nova will not be able to make entries for the IPTable rules, which might be required in order for the newly created instance to be able communicate to the Internet. Secondly, it is important to enable IP forwarding and making it persistent by using the configuration file /etc/sysctl.conf. Also, on CentOS, the following command can be executed:

```
echo 1 > /proc/sys/net/ipv4/ip_forward
```

Error received during installation – Unable to write random state

If the OpenStack installation script (such as stack.sh) is run as a root user then it can cause such an error because the ownership of the folder ~/.rnd is changed to the user root, and hence, a normal user (owning the home directory) cannot write to it.

It is recommended that you run the installation script (stack.sh) as a non-root user.

Timeout error received while running jeos_create during customization

It has been found that the `libvirt` network interface will be wedged somehow, if the `oz` command is run several times. A working network is needed by `oz` in order to update the virtual machine with `cloud-init` and several other package updates. A solution to this problem can be to destroy and recreate the network. More details on this issue can be seen at (813853) (`https://bugzilla.redhat.com/show_bug.cgi?id=813853`):

```
sudo virsh net-destroy default
sudo virsh net-start default
```

If the preceding solution does not solve the issue, then one reason could be one or more zombie `dnsmasq` processes.

During `oz` customization, the `virsh` console command can be used to log into the virtual machine using credentials `root/ozrootpw`.

A template running with incorrect parameters cannot be deleted

There is a known bug in Heat where templates are stored into databases before they are actually executed. If there are exception errors during creation, then there is a problem. Till this bug is fixed, there is a work around solution to drop the Heat dataset and recreating it:

```
killall -9 heat-api
killall -9 heat-engine
tools/heat-db-drop -r <mysql root password>
heat-manage db_sync
```

Error – internal error process exited while connecting to monitor

In some cases, `jeos_create` fails to create an image. The command used to create a JeOS image is as follows:

```
sudo -E heat jeos_create F16 x86_64 cfntools
```

The error may look something like the following screenshot:

```
Creating JEOS image (F16-x86_64-cfntools) - this takes approximately 10 minutes.

ERROR: internal error process exited while connecting to monitor: qemu-system-x86_64: -
netdev tap,fd=30,id=hostnet0,vhost=on,vhostfd=31: vhost-net support is not compiled in
qemu-system-x86_64: -netdev tap,fd=30,id=hostnet0,vhost=on,vhostfd=31: vhost-net reques
ted but could not be initialized
qemu-system-x86_64: -netdev tap,fd=30,id=hostnet0,vhost=on,vhostfd=31: Device 'tap' cou
ld not be initialized


(use -d3 to get the full backtrace)

oz-install did not create the image, check your oz installation.
```

CPU virtualization needs to be enabled in the bios of the host machine to solve this issue.

It takes too long to create a JeOS

OZ normally takes some time to complete. It is an issue if we need to run it multiple times in a testing/development environment. Some parameters can be tweaked in the /etc/oz.cfg file to speed up this process; however, this may result in higher disk usage on the system.

```
[cache]
original_media = yes
modified_media=yes
jeos=yes
```

Error – Quota exceeded: code=InstanceLimitExceeded (HTTP 413)

It is important to make sure that there are no non-deleted resources. Use the command mentioned in the following screenshot to list the available resources:

```
ubuntu@ubuntu:~$ nova list
+--------------------------------------+-----------+--------+------------------------+
|                  ID                  |   Name    | Status |        Networks        |
+--------------------------------------+-----------+--------+------------------------+
| 3b214c99-649a-4efc-9a92-01c4576b4ab2 | cirros VM | ACTIVE | cloudlivenet=172.20.1.2 |
+--------------------------------------+-----------+--------+------------------------+
```

To view our volumes attached to running instances, we use the following command:

```
nova volume-list
```

If this is not the case, then we need to check the quota limits or increase if needed. Current quotas can be displayed using the following command:

```
nova-manage project quota admin
```

The number of instances can be increased using:

```
nova-manage project quota admin --key=instances --value=100
```

Error – Response from Keystone does not contain a Heat endpoint

The error message may look something like this:

```
ubuntu@ubuntu:~$ heat list

ERROR:Failed to list. Got error:
ERROR:Response from Keystone does not contain a Heat endpoint.
```

It seems like the keystone configuration needs to set properly. The following actions can be taken to solve this issue:

```
heat-keystone-create endpoint
heat-keystone-create-devstack
```

It can also be caused if the credentials file is not properly sourced.

Error – Internal Server Error

If an error similar to the following is displayed:

```
ubuntu@ubuntu:~$ heat list

ERROR:Failed to list. Got error:
ERROR:Internal Server error: Internal Server Error
```

The backtrace may look something like this:

```
  File "/usr/lib64/python2.7/site-packages/sqlalchemy/engine/strategies.py", line 80, in connect
returndialect.connect(*cargs, **cparams)
  File "/usr/lib64/python2.7/site-packages/sqlalchemy/engine/default.py", line 281, in connect
returnself.dbapi.connect(*cargs, **cparams)
  File "/usr/lib64/python2.7/site-packages/MySQLdb/__init__.py", line 81, in Connect
return Connection(*args, **kwargs)
  File "/usr/lib64/python2.7/site-packages/MySQLdb/connections.py", line 187, in __init__
super(Connection, self).__init__(*args, **kwargs2)
OperationalError: (OperationalError) (1045, "Access denied for user 'heat'@'localhost' (using pass
word: YES)") None None
.
------------------------------------------
```

Running `heat-db-setup` may solve this issue.

Error – Provided KeyName is not registered with Nova

If the following error is received after creating a Heat template:

```
DEBUG:Debug level logging enabled
<CreateStackResult>
<ValidateTemplateResult>
<Description>Malformed Query Response {'Error': 'Provided KeyName is not registered with nova'}
</Description>
<Parameters/>
</ValidateTemplateResult>
</CreateStackResult>
```

The SSH keys need to be registered with Nova compute, to solve this issue. The OpenStack quick start guide is available at (http://docs.openstack.org/developer/horizon/quickstart.html) can be helpful in this regard.

A template is not working after editing

It's easy to introduce JSON syntax errors when editing templates, so this can be useful to identify what/where is broken:

```
ubuntu@ubuntu:~$ cat foo.template | python -m json.tool

Expecting , delimiter: line 107 column 20 (char 4579)
```

Nova starts creating instances that immediately go to the ERROR state. If it is observed that instances are not being created properly and if the command nova list shows ERROR state, then it will be necessary to check the scheduler log.

The following is a sample error message displayed under /var/log/nova/scheduler.log:

```
2012-08-02 15:29:34 WARNING nova.scheduler.manager [req-f7ea2e26-3c92-49a4-9610-c59216bb8111 af
787dc6ab8a48a392aa5ddbbef38073 bf80a27b120e46bda2cb64e0123fea27] Failed to schedule_run_instanc
e: No valid host was found.

2012-08-02 15:29:34 WARNING nova.scheduler.manager [req-f7ea2e26-3c92-49a4-9610-c59216bb8111 af
787dc6ab8a48a392aa5ddbbef38073 bf80a27b120e46bda2cb64e0123fea27] Setting instance 18165ff9-25ae
-4d01-8761-f414c86a0a64 to ERROR state.
```

To solve this problem, it is necessary to set the Nova configuration file (/etc/nova.conf) as follows:

```
scheduler_default_filters=AllHostsFilter
```

For further details, visit the following URL:

https://answers.launchpad.net/nova/+question/192511

Instances shutdown immediately after creation

If the Nova compute logs show an error in which the instances go to the error state right away, then it means that QEMU has failed to launch the new instance. There can be more than one thing causing this issue, and insufficient memory can be one of them.

The following is a sample error displayed under the instance log:

```
ubuntu@ubuntu:~$ tail -n2 /var/log/libvirt/qemu/instance-00000003.log
Failed to allocate 17179869184 B: Cannot allocate memory
2012-08-02 15:18:18.101+0000: shutting down
```

Yum update fails with dependency problems related to the oz package

If oz was built from the Git repository, as described in the installation guides, then apt-get update (on Ubuntu) of yum update (CentOS) will fail due to dependency problems while updating the Python packages for OS.

This is because the package (for oz) built locally also needs to be updated to match the Python version. The solution is to remove the package, and then install it again after doing a system update:

```
sudo yum remove oz
sudo yum update
# rebuild OZ as detailed in the getting started guide
cd ~/git/oz/
git pull
rm -f ~/rpmbuild/RPMS/noarch/oz-*
make rpm
sudo yum localinstall ~/rpmbuild/RPMS/noarch/oz-*.rpm
```

 For Ubuntu, please refer to the installation guide.

Failed to start qpidd

The service scripts (for starting and stopping qpiddaemon) have been moved to qpid-cpp-server-daemon package as of qpid-cpp-server 0.16-5.

If the system was updated from an earlier qpid-cpp-server version, then it may fail while starting OpenStack, giving an error like this:

```
ubunutu@ubunut:~$ ./tools/openstack restart
Failed to issue method call: Unit qpidd.service failed to load: No such file or directory. See
system logs and 'systemctl status qpidd.service' for details.
```

The solution is to reinstall the updated version of qpid-cpp-server-daemon, and then start or restart OpenStack:

```
yum install qpid-cpp-server-daemon
tools/openstack restart
```

OpenStack daemons can't connect to qpidd

If OpenStack components are not able to connect to the qipdd and if the error message displays: "Address family for hostname not supported," then it means the problem is with the IP configuration on one of the interfaces.

```
2012-10-31 22:54:11    DEBUG [qpid.messaging.io.raw] OPEN[216d758]: localhost:5672
2012-10-31 22:54:11  WARNING [qpid.messaging] recoverable error[attempt 1]: [Errno -9] Address
family for hostname not supported
2012-10-31 22:54:11  WARNING [qpid.messaging] sleeping 1 seconds
```

This can happen if IPv6 is enabled and the loopback interface (lo0) does not have a valid IPv6 address. The problem can be solved by editing the /etc/hosts file:

`vi /etc/hosts`

`# "::1"`

 The preceding line needs to be commented using #.

Ubuntu VMs cannot receive DHCP assignments from hosts running CentOS/Fedora

DHCP assignment failure can be caused if firewall is blocking the DHCP traffic. The firewall (IPTable) rule needs to be added as follows:

```
iptables -A POSTROUTING -t mangle -p udp --dport 68 -j CHECKSUM
--checksum-fill
```

Debugging OpenStack Heat

The Heat CLI can be used to execute commands and check the status of Heat components. In this regard, the most useful method is to use the Heat CLI.

The Heat list command can be used to check the Heat state on the node.

Heat list returns 503 error

The credentials inside OpenStack Heat configuration files (under `/etc/heat`) may be incorrect. The Heat username and password need to be correctly specified under Heat configuration files.

Heat list hangs up

If the command `heat list` is taking very long and hangs up, then this means that connection to the messaging server (RabbitMQ) has not been established correctly.

Troubleshooting common OpenStack errors

First of all, check that all Nova services are in a stable state:

```
$nova-manage service list
Binary Host Zone Status State Updated_At
nova-scheduler openstack1 nova enabled : - ) 2012-05-12 22:42:14
nova-compute openstack1 nova enabled : - ) 2012-05-12 22:42:12
nova-network openstack1 nova enabled : - ) 2012-05-12 22:42:14
```

Secondly, check that all nova processes are running:

```
$ ps -ea | grep nova
11448 ? 00:02:54 nova-cert
12072 ? 00:02:57 nova-network
12083 ? 00:10:31 nova-compute
12093 ? 00:06:40 nova-api
12117 ? 00:02:26 nova-scheduler
12154 ? 00:00:00 nova-xvpvncprox
55746 ? 00:00:00 nova-objectstor
```

For further insight into any errors, the log files are very helpful. The following command can be used to see the logs files:

```
$tail -n 400 /var/log/nova-compute
```

Error – internal error Failed to create mDNS client: Daemon not running

The following is the error output displayed while starting the `libvirt` daemon:

```
python2.7/dist-packages/nova/virt/libvirt/connection.py", line 338, in _connect
2012-05-09 17:05:42 TRACE nova return libvirt.openAuth(uri, auth, 0)
2012-05-09 17:05:42 TRACE nova File "/usr/lib/python2.7/dist-packages/libvirt.py", line 102, in
 openAuth
2012-05-09 17:05:42 TRACE nova if ret is None:raiselibvirtError('virConnectOpenAuth() failed')
2012-05-09 17:05:42 TRACE nova libvirtError: Failed to connect socket to '/var/run/libvirt/libv
irt-sock': No such file or directory
012-05-09 22:05:41.909+0000: 12466: info : libvirt version: 0.9.8
2012-05-09 22:05:41.909+0000: 12466: error : virNetServerMDNSStart:460 : internal error Failed
to create mDNS client: Daemon not running
```

The solution

The problem is that the `libvirt-bin` service will not start without `dbus` installed. The solution is to install `lxc`.

Also, staring the `dbus` service will be helpful:

```
sudo apt-get install lxc
```

Error – Failed to add image

If you receive an error message like the following:

```
Error: Failed to add image. Got error: The request returned 500 Internal
Server Error
```

Then the solution is to check the credentials file for any errors. Alternatively, you can fix the OS ENV variables (substitute the usernames and passwords accordingly):

```
declare -x OS_AUTH_KEY="openstack"

declare -x OS_AUTH_URL="http://localhost:5000/v2.0/"

declare -x OS_PASSWORD="openstack"

declare -x OS_TENANT_NAME="admin"

declare -x OS_USERNAME="admin"Nova Instance Not Found
```

If you receive an error that contains a message like the following in the `libvirt.log` file:

```
2012-05-09 17:58:08 TRACE nova raiseexception.InstanceNotFound(instance_id=instance_name)
2012-05-09 17:58:08 TRACE nova InstanceNotFound: Instance instance-00000002 could not be found.
```

Then perform the following steps:

1. Either delete the instance in MySQL or drop the database and start a new one. The following commands can be used:

   ```
   $mysql -u root -p

   DROP DATABASE nova;

   Recreate the DB:

   CREATE DATABASE nova; (strip formatting if you copy and paste any
   of this)

   GRANT ALL PRIVILEGES ON nova.* TO 'novadbadmin'@'%' IDENTIFIED

   BY '<password>';

   Quit
   ```

2. The next step is to sync the database using the following command:

   ```
   $nova-manage db sync
   ```

3. Finally, restart Nova:

   ```
   ubuntu@ubuntu:~$ for a in libvirt-bin nova-network nova-compute nova-api nova-objectstore nova-
   scheduler nova-volume nova-vncproxy; do service "$a" stop; done

   ubuntu@ubuntu:~$ for a in libvirt-bin nova-network nova-compute nova-api nova-objectstore nova-
   scheduler nova-volume nova-vncproxy; do service "$a" start; done
   ```

4. Now, regenerate the ssh keys using the following command:

   ```
   $nova keypair-add ssh_key>ssh_key.pem
   ```

5. Then, reapply the security policy:

   ```
   $nova secgroup-add-rule default icmp -1 -1 0.0.0.0/0

   $nova secgroup-add-rule default tcp 22 22 0.0.0.0/0
   ```

6. Then, clean the artifacts of the old and unused instances using the following command:

   ```
   ubuntu@ubuntu:~$ rm -rf /etc/libvirt/qemu/instance-00000043.xml
   ubuntu@ubuntu:~$ rm -rf /etc/libvirt/qemu/instance-00000043.monitor
   ubuntu@ubuntu:~$ rm -rf /etc/libvirt/qemu/instance-00000043/console.log
   ubuntu@ubuntu:~$ rm -rf /etc/libvirt/qemu/instance-00000043/disk
   ubuntu@ubuntu:~$ rm -rf /etc/libvirt/qemu/instance-00000043/libvirt.xml
   ubuntu@ubuntu:~$ rm -rf /etc/libvirt/qemu/instance-00000043.log
   ```

7. Restart the `libvirt` daemon and check the logs again for any errors:

```
Service libvirt-bin restart

tail -n 200 cat /var/log/libvirt/libvirtd.log
```

While configuring Heat, I accidently removed some Nova files. In this case, we need to rebuild Nova using the following commands:

```
apt-get purge nova-api nova-cert nova-common nova-compute nova-compute-
kvm nova-doc nova-network nova-objectstore nova-scheduler nova-vncproxy
nova-volume python-nova python-novaclient

mysqlshow -count glance

$rm -rf /root/.novaclient/

$rm -rf /var/lib/nova

$rm -rf /var/lib/mysql/nova

$rm -rf /etc/libvirt/nwfilter/nova*

MySQL -u name -r

Drop database nova;

CREATE DATABASE nova;

GRANT ALL PRIVILEGES ON nova.* TO 'novadbadmin'@'%'

IDENTIFIED BY 'openstack';

killalldnsmasq

service nova-network restart

ps -ea | grep key

ps -ea | grep nova

ps -ea | grepgl

root@openstack:/home/openstack# apt-get install -y mysql-server python-
mysqldbmysql-common


apt-get install nova-api nova-cert nova-common nova-compute nova-compute-
kvm nova-doc nova-network nova-objectstore nova-scheduler nova-vncproxy
nova-volume python-nova python-novaclient
```

Also, you need to verify the following log files:

```
/var/log/nova/nova-api.log
/var/log/nova/nova-cert.log
/var/log/nova/nova-compute.log
/var/log/nova/nova-dhcpbridge.log
/var/log/nova/nova-manage.log
/var/log/nova/nova-network.log
```

```
/var/log/nova/nova-objectstore.log
/var/log/nova/nova-scheduler.log
/var/log/nova/nova-volume.log
/var/log/nova/nova-xvpvncproxy.log
/var/log/upstart/nova-api.log
/var/log/upstart/nova-cert.log
/var/log/upstart/nova-compute.log
/var/log/upstart/nova-network.log
/var/log/upstart/nova-objectstore.log
/var/log/upstart/nova-scheduler.log
/var/log/upstart/nova-vncproxy.log
/var/log/upstart/nova-volume.log
/var/crash/_usr_bin_nova-api.114.crash
/var/crash/_usr_bin_nova-compute.114.crash
/var/crash/_usr_bin_nova-network.114.crash
/var/crash/_usr_bin_nova-objectstore.114.crash
/var/crash/_usr_bin_nova-scheduler.114.crash
/var/crash/_usr_bin_nova-xvpvncproxy.114.crash
```

Keystone ValueError – you need to pass either an existing engine or a database uri

The error details may contain something like this:

```
File "/usr/lib/python2.7/dist-packages/migrate/versioning/util/__
init__.py", line 116, in construct_engine
raise ValueError("you need to pass either an existing engine or a
database uri")
ValueError: you need to pass either an existing engine or a database
uri
```

Verify that the following line is present in the keystone configuration file
(/etc/keystone.conf):

```
connection = mysql://keystone:openstack@localhost:3306/keystone
```

Error – No handlers could be found for logger keystoneclient.client

The error shown is: No handlers could be found for logger
'keystoneclient.client' Authorization Failed: Unable to communicate
with identity service: '\xe2\x80\x9dhttp'. (HTTP 400).

The solution is to export the correct credentials to the environment.

```
ubuntu@ubuntu:~$ export SERVICE_TOKEN=openstack
ubuntu@ubuntu:~$ export OS_TENANT_NAME=admin
ubuntu@ubuntu:~$ export OS_USERNAME=admin
ubuntu@ubuntu:~$ export OS_PASSWORD=openstack
ubuntu@ubuntu:~$ export OS_AUTH_URL="http://localhost:5000/v2.0/"
ubuntu@ubuntu:~$ export SERVICE_ENDPOINT=http://localhost:35357/v2.0
```

Another requirement is to verify that the correct tokens are being used in `keystone.conf` file. If required, open the file: `/etc/keystone/keystone.conf` and make sure that the following configuration is present:

```
driver = keystone.catalog.backends.templated.TemplatedCatalog
template_file = /etc/keystone/default_catalog.templates
```

Next, we verify that the credentials that we exported earlier are working using the following command:

```
# keystone user-list
+----------------------------------+------------+---------+-------+
|                id                |    name    | enabled | email |
+----------------------------------+------------+---------+-------+
| 390f2da1b41447aea3fa87f3feb77159 |   admin    |  True   |       |
| e2d55836f1d64e7d9131eedb222803ea |   cinder   |  True   |       |
| 690ba1fd20104b7db99873c02d7497a3 |   glance   |  True   |       |
| 62b9f4c6924749deb80c2f3e0ed86df8 | monitoring |  True   |       |
| 3b57d891ef9649c087d6c7259f0cdf80 |    nova    |  True   |       |
+----------------------------------+------------+---------+-------+
```

Error – Access denied for user 'keystone'@'openstack1' (using password: YES)

If the error details look something like this:

```
File "/usr/lib/python2.7/dist-packages/MySQLdb/connections.py", line
187, in __init__
super(Connection, self).__init__(*args, **kwargs2)
sqlalchemy.exc.OperationalError: (OperationalError) (1045, "Access
denied for user 'keystone'@'openstack1 (using password: YES)") None
None
```

It is necessary to make sure that the `keystone.conf` file looks like this:

```
[sql]
connection = mysql://keystone:openstack@localhost:3306/keystone
```

Error – Connect error/bad request to Auth service at URL %(url)s

The solution to the problem is to verify that proper service endpoints have been defined in the keystone and also OS_AUTH_URL has been properly exported.

```
export SERVICE_TOKEN=openstack
export OS_TENANT_NAME=admin
export OS_USERNAME=admin
export OS_PASSWORD=openstack
export OS_AUTH_URL=http://localhost:5000/v2.0/
export SERVICE_ENDPOINT=http://localhost:35357/v2.0
```

Summary

In this chapter, we looked at a few issues faced while running and managing OpenStack Heat. We have tried to address a few well-known issues and discussed troubleshooting the errors received.

Mostly, such issues are due to missing parameters in the associated configuration files or typing mistakes. However, there are a few known bugs, which are still without resolution by the Heat developers' team. The Heat website and relevant documentations can be used to get an up-to-date status of bugs and their fixes.

The following is a list of useful links where more information can be found relating to Heat and other OpenStack components:

- http://docs.openstack.org/
- http://docs.openstack.org/user-guide-admin/
- http://docs.openstack.org/ops

Index

A

Amazon CloudFormation
  features 70
application programming interface (API) 13
authorization model configuration 6
autoscaling
  about 37
  horizontal scaling 38
  vertical scaling 37
  with Heat 39
autoscaling, with Heat
  about 39
  high availability 40, 41
  stateless, versus stateful services 41
  working 39, 40

C

CloudFormation-compatible
      format (CFN) 33
CloudFormation template
  AWS template format version 109
  Conditions section 109
  deleting 108
  Description parameter 109
  Mappings section 109
  Metadata section 109
  Outputs section 110
  Parameters section 109
  Resources section 109
command-line interface, for Heat
  help screen, displaying 74-76
  using 73

D

Database as a Service (DBaaS) 3
DevStack
  defining 97-103
  drawback 97

E

event stack list
  defining 103, 104
example architecture
  based on Neutron 22-24
  based on Nova network 20
example architecture,
      based on Nova network
  detailed description 21, 22
  Node hardware specifications 20
  overview 20

G

Glance 3

H

Heat
  about 3, 31
  basics 31, 32
  TOSCA (Topology and Orchestration
      Specification for Cloud Applications) 3
Heat basics
  CFN 32
  Heat Orchestration Template (HOT) 33

Thank you for buying
OpenStack Orchestration

About Packt Publishing

Packt, pronounced 'packed', published its first book, *Mastering phpMyAdmin for Effective MySQL Management*, in April 2004, and subsequently continued to specialize in publishing highly focused books on specific technologies and solutions.

Our books and publications share the experiences of your fellow IT professionals in adapting and customizing today's systems, applications, and frameworks. Our solution-based books give you the knowledge and power to customize the software and technologies you're using to get the job done. Packt books are more specific and less general than the IT books you have seen in the past. Our unique business model allows us to bring you more focused information, giving you more of what you need to know, and less of what you don't.

Packt is a modern yet unique publishing company that focuses on producing quality, cutting-edge books for communities of developers, administrators, and newbies alike. For more information, please visit our website at www.packtpub.com.

About Packt Open Source

In 2010, Packt launched two new brands, Packt Open Source and Packt Enterprise, in order to continue its focus on specialization. This book is part of the Packt Open Source brand, home to books published on software built around open source licenses, and offering information to anybody from advanced developers to budding web designers. The Open Source brand also runs Packt's Open Source Royalty Scheme, by which Packt gives a royalty to each open source project about whose software a book is sold.

Writing for Packt

We welcome all inquiries from people who are interested in authoring. Book proposals should be sent to author@packtpub.com. If your book idea is still at an early stage and you would like to discuss it first before writing a formal book proposal, then please contact us; one of our commissioning editors will get in touch with you.

We're not just looking for published authors; if you have strong technical skills but no writing experience, our experienced editors can help you develop a writing career, or simply get some additional reward for your expertise.

OpenStack Essentials

ISBN: 978-1-78398-708-5   Paperback: 168 pages

Demystify the cloud by building your own private OpenStack cloud

1. Set up a powerful cloud platform using OpenStack.

2. Learn about the components of OpenStack and how they interact with each other.

3. Follow a step-by-step process that exposes the inner details of an OpenStack cluster.

OpenStack Cloud Computing Cookbook
Third Edition

ISBN: 978-1-78217-478-3   Paperback: 436 pages

Over 110 effective recipes to help you build and operate OpenStack cloud computing, storage, networking, and automation

1. Explore many new features of OpenStack's Juno and Kilo releases.

2. Install, configure, and administer core projects with the help of OpenStack Object Storage, Block Storage, and Neutron Networking services.

Please check **www.PacktPub.com** for information on our titles